DESTINED
I.V.A.

DAUGHTERS OF INTEGRITY, VIRTUE & ANOINTING

*Leading Teen Girls
in the Way of Christ*

LEADER'S GUIDE

25 SESSIONS
Interactive Format

LAURA E. KNIGHTS, MSW

All scripture quotations, unless otherwise indicated, are taken from the Holy Bible, New International Version®, NIV®. Copyright ©1973, 1978, 1984, 2011 by Biblica, Inc.™ Used by permission of Zondervan. All rights reserved worldwide. www.zondervan.com The "NIV" and "New International Version" are trademarks registered in the United States Patent and Trademark Office by Biblica, Inc.™

Scripture quotations marked (NLT) are taken from the Holy Bible, New Living Translation, copyright © 1996, 2004, 2007 by Tyndale House Foundation. Used by permission of Tyndale House Publishers, Inc., Carol Stream, Illinois 60188. All rights reserved.

All Scripture quotations in this publication are from THE MESSAGE. Copyright © by Eugene H. Peterson 1993, 1994, 1995, 1996, 2000, 2001, 2002. Used by permission of NavPress Publishing Group.

Published by NyreePress Publishing
a division of NyreePress Literary Group
www.nyreepress.com
To order bulk copies, contact NyreePress:
972-793-3736
info@nyreepress.com

Library of Congress Control Number: 2013946107
Knights, Laura E.
      Destined D.I.V.A.: Daughters of Integrity, Virtue, and Anointing, Leader's Guide/ by Laura E. Knights
      Teen / Inspirational / Christian Living
ISBN (sc) 978-0-9890039-4-0

Cover design by Bezworks Designs, LLC
Printed in the United States of America.

Laura E. Knights, MSW
laura@thedestineddivas.com
www.thedestineddivas.com
www.lauraeknights.com

DEDICATION

To my parents,
Leon and Elizabeth Rogers, Sr.
who raised me to be a Destined D.I.V.A., and showed me the love of Jesus Christ
in both word and deed.

To my husband and love of my life, Marshall, and our daughter, Kai, who have patiently shared
me with this process. I love you always.

Foreword

The Destined D.I.V.A. Leader's Guide is a very well written manual to accompany a thoroughly planned program. From its inception up to this point, it has undoubtedly required Laura Knights to diligently seek God for direction and confirmation of purpose. I can see that the Leader's Guide has been designed to advance Christ-like behaviors in young women by setting sound and rigorous standards for everyday living. Laura has sought to establish a simple set of rules that would codify the many aspects of a young girl's journey into womanhood to increase the ease of saying no to the flesh and yes to God.

Through an easy-to-follow template, other virtuous women who have a heart for God and teen girls will be able to start Destined D.I.V.A. groups in their own churches, communities, and families. Whereas a single bible-based empowerment group for girls is useful and necessary to impact the girls within one's reach; the Destined D.I.V.A. system allows for women across the nation, across the world even, to be empowered to serve girls right where there are. What a blessing! The Destined D.I.V.A. system expands the influence of women, and their reach to teen girls, to nurture and develop girls into virtuous women of God. Through sessions on topics ranging from accepting salvation, learning how to pray, building self-esteem, and dealing with sexual temptation; Laura Knights provides an opportunity for women to be of service to teen girls, who so desperately need their Godly mentoring and guidance, in a fun and exciting format that will keep girls interested and engaged.

I have seen the positive impact of the Destined D.I.V.A. Lifestyle System on the girls in our church, and even girls that have come to join the group from the surrounding community. During my tenure as Pastor of Mary Magdalene Baptist Church, and under divine leadership by Laura Knights, I have watched the Destined D.I.V.A. program grow from a visionary's seed into a program that has potential to impact thousands of girls' lives for the rest their natural life and beyond. This profusion of wisdom has been and continues to be supported and defined by the guidance provided by the Holy Spirit. With the Word of God as its foundation, the Destined D.I.V.A. system is helping to establish a solid base upon which the girls in our church are building bright futures for themselves and a stronger, more powerful body of Christ.

Rev. Stephen Henry, Senior Pastor
Mary Magdalene Baptist Church
10920 S. Princeton Avenue
Chicago, IL 60628

Contents

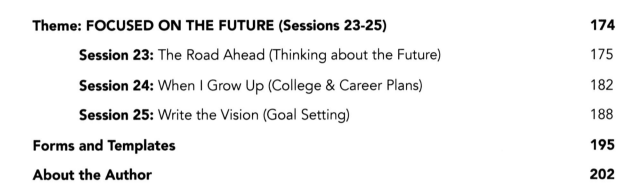

Acknowledgments

Let me start by saying that God and God alone knows what the completion of this project means to me. This process has truly been a journey and a labor of love. After eight 'girl empowerment groups' in various incarnations over the years, and two years of writing and leading a Destined D.I.V.A. group, I am overjoyed to be at this stage of the journey. I have grown in so many ways– spiritually and *emotionally*—while working on this project. Many people have assisted me along this journey, and their presence in my life really made a difference. I am forever grateful.

To my wonderful husband and best friend, Marshall: Thank you for your support, patience, and encouragement throughout this entire journey.

To our sweet girl, Kai, who has been curious about my "work" and who has always reminded me in her special way that my first priority is being a wife and mom. Mommy loves you so much! You are my favorite girl!

To my parents who have always supported me in every endeavor: Mom, thank you for being my first investor. You showed me in word and in deed that only the things we do for Christ will last. Dad, even in your passing, you taught me so much about God's grace and the importance of spirituality, not religion.

To my sisters, Lisa and Bridgette, who watched my child so that I could have extended periods to write: Thank you for your love and support.

To my Pastor, Rev. Stephen Henry, who gave me the opportunity to start a Destined D.I.V.A. group at our church, and encouraged me at each step to continue to make disciples of the teen girls I served: Thank you for the opportunity.

To Dr. Tyvette Hilliard, my "sister from another mother" and Destined D.I.V.A. Co-Leader: Your dependable presence spoke volumes to me and the girls. I am inspired by your example.

To Jonnitra Bland, an awesome woman of God: Thank you for your time, attention, and support to read this book, and study on my behalf to help me "rightly divide the Word." Your insights were priceless and caused me to dig deeper in my own study of God's Word.

And last, but certainly not least…to my Destined D.I.V.A.s – Lizzie, Britney, Kristen, Patrice, Jade, Kishandra, Samantha, Kaitlyn, Chauntay, Chiquita, Darnecia, Briana, Kiesha, Nina, and Crystal: Thank you for allowing God to use me in your lives. Your triumphs and challenges have taught me so much about God's love, sisterhood, faith, determination, hope, joy, and so much more. I am honored to play a small role in leading you in the way of Christ. I look forward with great anticipation to see the wonderful harvest God will show through you. Love you girls! D.I.V.A.s rock!

Reproducible Handouts

Session 1: Laying the Foundation
- Destined D.I.V.A. Acronym Handout

Session 2: Extreme Makeover (Salvation)
- Salvation Illustration
- Extreme Makeover Worksheet

Session 5: New Identity (Dead to Self, Alive in Christ)
- If They Really Knew Me Worksheet

Session 6: Take off the Mask (Staying True to Self)
- Take off the Mask Worksheet

Session 7: Walking with Christ (Commitment to Christ)
- Which Shoes Are You Wearing? Activity

Session 8: Decisions, Decisions (Choices and Decision Making)
- Ready, Think, Action! Scenarios
- Steps for Responsible Decision-Making Worksheet
- Steps for Responsible Decision-Making Reminder Cards

Session 9: What's on Your Tree? (Fruits of the Spirit)
- Fruits of the Spirit Signs
- What's on Your Tree? Worksheet

Session 12: Seeing Red (Dealing with Anger)
- Seeing Red Anger Scale Worksheet
- How do you Deal? Scenarios

Session 13: Follow the Leader (Servant Leadership)
- Serving It Up! Worksheet

Session 15: So Fresh & So Clean (Personal Hygiene)
- Tips to Stay So Fresh & So Clean Handout
- Personal Hygiene Jeopardy Answer Key

Session 16: Hold Out (Dealing with Sexual Temptation)
- Plan Your Purity Worksheet

Session 17: Garbage In, Garbage Out (Media Consumption)
- Garbage or Not? Activity Sheet

Session 19: Honor and Obey (Relationships with Parents)
- Letter to my Parents Worksheet

Session 20: Say What?!?! (Communication Skills & Power of Words)
- Say What?!?! Communication Tips Handout
- Say What?!?! Role Play Scenarios

Session 21: Say It Loud (Sharing Our Faith)
- Say It Loud Cards

Session 22: Give Thanks, Give Back (Community Service)
- Service Illustration Handout
- Service Brainstorm Worksheet

Session 23: The Road Ahead (Thinking about the Future)
- My Dream Plan Worksheet
- View of the Past Worksheet

Session 24: Write the Vision (Goal Setting)
- College & Career Planning Worksheet
- Silly Group Review

Session 25: When I Grow Up (College & Career Plans)
- Writing SMART Goals Worksheet

Introduction

Destined D.I.V.A. is a concept that's been on my heart for some time. Over the last 10 years, I have facilitated several prayer, psychosocial, and life skills groups for young women and teen girls in spiritual, educational, and therapeutic settings. The groups have taken on several forms, but the format used for this curriculum was solidified in 2011 through a group I facilitate at my church, Mary Magdalene M.B. Church in Chicago, Illinois (Senior Pastor, Rev. Stephen Henry). Through the group, I have been able to witness firsthand the growth in the young women that I work with, and it has been such a blessing to see them become stronger at verbalizing their faith and gaining convictions about how they are living their lives.

When I discussed the group with other women, several would share about their own desire to do something similar in their churches, communities, and families but they just did not know where to start or how to put a "lesson" together that would interest and engage teen girls. Additionally, consistent feedback from women that I talked to led me to believe that this curriculum could be a gift for others to use with teen girls everywhere. I have always had a passion for working with teen girls, and in these times with incessant spiritual attacks on our youth, the need for a safe space for girls to learn about God, themselves, and why they so desperately need Him is of utmost importance.

The Destined D.I.V.A. Leader's Guide is a scripture-based curriculum for teen girls, ages 13-18, with a focus on teaching life skills and biblical truths that will help young women make positive decisions that are aligned with their identity as children of God. The curriculum was created to be facilitated by adult women in a small group setting.

The Destined D.I.V.A. sessions are designed to combine Bible study, prayer, group discussion, life skills, interactive activities (i.e. role plays, games, etc.), and personal reflection with mentoring from adult women that are non-judgmental and transparent in their experiences on their own Christian journey. While developing this curriculum, the scriptural references that were always on my heart included:

Before I formed you in the womb I knew you, before you were born I set you apart; I appointed you as a prophet to the nations. (Jeremiah 1:5)

For I know the plans I have for you," declares the LORD, "plans to prosper you and not to harm you, plans to give you hope and a future (Jeremiah 29:11)

But you are a chosen people, a royal priesthood, a holy nation, God's special possession, that you may declare the praises of him who called you out of darkness into his wonderful light. (1 Peter 2:9)

Through the Destined D.I.V.A. sessions, teen girls are empowered through God's Word to stand out of the crowd, embrace their identity as disciples of Christ, and walk in God's love to let their light shine.

The Destined D.I.V.A. Acronym

Destined – ordained, appointed, or predetermined to be or do something

Daughters – of Christ and wonderfully beheld in His eyes

Integrity – complete, undivided, and adhering to Christian values; committed to letting our words match our actions

Virtue – full of beautiful attributes and having the power to put them into action

Anointing – chosen and filled with God's power

Although my original intention for doing this ministry work had not included developing a curriculum, I was praying about an entrepreneurial endeavor that would tie together my passion for working with women and girls, my faith, and my background as a social worker and youth development specialist. My prayers were answered, and The Destined D.I.V.A. Lifestyle System was birthed. In addition to this leader's guide, the Destined D.I.V.A. product line includes the D.I.V.A. handbook for teen girls, D.I.V.A. Leader trainings, the annual Destined D.I.V.A. Expo, and other D.I.V.A. Live! events and signature talks for teen girls and women. Also, as a leader, you can sign up for the D.I.V.A. Mail blog and quarterly e-newsletter to receive up-to-date information and encouraging words to inspire you on this journey. Learn more about these offerings at www.thedestineddivas.com.

Why Destined D.I.V.A.?

Gender specific ministry with modeling from adult women is crucial to developing girls into women of God. From broken families, misogyny in media, and communities in turmoil; girls are faced with so many mixed-messages, temptations, and negative images on a daily basis. Positive adult relationships rooted in biblical modeling provide girls with a safe space to express feelings and learn biblical truths. Information obtained about real life issues can help them grow in their personal relationship with Christ, as well as find answers to the issues they are facing in their life. Additionally, girls learn how to cultivate sisterhood and peer support that will lead to strong, lasting friendships. The Destined D.I.V.A. curriculum, facilitated in its intended format, provides a safe space filled with God's love to reaffirm their self-esteem and combat negative influences.

The Destined D.I.V.A. curriculum helps schools, churches, organizations, families, and other ministries:

- Minister God's Word to girls through consistent Bible study/discussion groups, and individual and group mentoring by women leaders

- Support and encourage girls in their personal decision to accept Christ as their Lord and Savior, and support their growth as they develop a personal relationship with Him

- Encourage teen girls to grow in their spiritual identity as children of God, and help them understand what it means to develop a personal relationship with Him

- Provide a space for girls to interact with and encourage each other through regular meetings, social outings, and service projects.

- Educate girls on life skill issues such as self-esteem, healthy relationships, sexuality, goal setting, anger management, leadership, and stress management to help them make healthy choices.

Statement of Faith

Although, I do not profess to be a biblical scholar, I have approached developing this curriculum with a mindset of searching and studying for my own growth. This is an honest, prayerful effort to show and share the profound blessings I have received from pouring into young women, just as Christian women have poured into me during my adolescence and in adulthood. The Destined D.I.V.A. curriculum and product line are based on the following tenets of the Christian faith:

There is one all knowing and all powerful God, existing in three persons (the Father, the Son and the Holy Spirit) that created the world and all of its contents.

For there are three that bear record in heaven, the Father, the Word, and the Holy Ghost: and these three are one. (1 John 5:7 King James Version)

Jesus is both completely man and God, and is the manifestation of God's word.

In the beginning was the Word, and the Word was with God, and the Word was God. The Word became flesh and made his dwelling among us. We have seen his glory, the glory of the one and only Son, who came from the Father, full of grace and truth. (John 1:1, 14)

Jesus Christ is the Messiah. He was born of a virgin through the Holy Spirit.

This is how the birth of Jesus the Messiah came about: His mother Mary was pledged to be married to Joseph, but before they came together, she was found to be pregnant through the Holy Spirit. (Matthew 1:18)

Jesus was crucified on the cross for our sins, was raised to life on the third day with all power, and ascended to heaven to sit at the right hand of God. This act served as blood atonement for our sins, and reconciled us to God because of His grace and mercy.

They brought Jesus to the place called

Golgotha (which means "the place of the skull"). Then they offered him wine mixed with myrrh, but he did not take it. And they crucified him. Dividing up his clothes, they cast lots to see what each would get. (Mark 15:22-24)

"Don't be alarmed," he said. "You are looking for Jesus the Nazarene, who was crucified. He has risen! He is not here. See the place where they laid him. (Mark 16:6)

Who then is the one who condemns? No one. Christ Jesus who died—more than that, who was raised to life—is at the right hand of God and is also interceding for us. (Romans 8:34)

Therefore, if anyone is in Christ, the new creation has come: The old has gone, the new is here! All this is from God, who reconciled us to himself through Christ and gave us the ministry of reconciliation: that God was reconciling the world to himself in Christ, not counting people's sins against them. And he has committed to us the message of reconciliation. We are therefore Christ's ambassadors, as though God were making his appeal through us. We implore you on Christ's behalf: Be reconciled to God. God made him who had no sin to be sin for us, so that in him we might become the righteousness of God. (2 Corinthians 5:17-21)

But because of his great love for us, God, who is rich in mercy, made us alive with Christ even when we were dead in transgressions—it is by grace you have been saved. (Ephesians 2:4)

Salvation and eternal life are received through accepting Jesus Christ as our Lord and Savior.

If you declare with your mouth, "Jesus is Lord," and believe in your heart that God raised him from the dead, you will be saved. (Romans 10:9)

Jesus answered, "I am the way and the truth and the life. No one comes to the Father except through me. If you really know me, you will know my Father as well. From now on, you do know him and have seen him." (John 14:6-7)

He who believes in the Son of God has the witness in himself; he who does not believe God has made Him a liar, because he has not believed the testimony that God has given of His Son. And this is the testimony: that God has given us eternal life, and this life is in His Son. (1 John 5:10-11)

The Holy Spirit leads, guides, and lives in us to help us to live according to God's word.

"If you love me, keep my commands. And I will ask the Father, and he will give you another advocate to help you and be with you forever— the Spirit of truth. The world cannot accept him, because it neither sees him nor knows him. But you know him, for he lives with you and will be in you. But the Advocate, the Holy Spirit, whom the Father will send in my name, will teach you all things and will remind you of everything I have said to you. (John 14:15-17, 21)

The bible is the Word of God and is an "instruction manual" for while we are here on earth.

All Scripture is God-breathed and is useful for teaching, rebuking, correcting and training in righteousness, so that the servant of God may be thoroughly equipped for every good work. (2 Timothy 3: 16-17)

Sanctification is the Goal

God is sovereign, but we have responsibility. We are the means in which God will reach out to these young women, yet it is He that will draw them unto Him.

All things have been committed to me by my Father. No one knows the Son except the Father, and no one knows the Father except the Son and those to whom the Son chooses to reveal him. (Matthew 11:27)

Given this, it is not our job to force young women to accept and follow Christ, but to share God's word and sow seeds that allow them to seek Him. Although we want to encourage the girls to accept Christ, we want to encourage more than just a verbal confession, but the evidence of sanctification. Sanctification is the process of growing in holiness and grace that occurs after accepting salvation. It takes time to develop. I was greatly inspired by a book entitled, *Gospel – Powered Parenting: How the Gospel Shapes and Transforms Parenting*, by William P. Farley, while putting the finishing touches on this curriculum. In his book, Farley gives a great explanation of

this concept of sanctification. He refers to this process "new birth:"

Even a child's testimony that he has "accepted Jesus" or "asked Jesus into his heart" means very little. That is because God initiates new birth. Of course, the child is responsible to respond to God with faith and repentance that point to new birth. New birth is a radical change of heart that ushers in new desires, new loves, and new life direction...It means that the child now owns Christianity for himself (pp. 28-29).

Farley goes on to say

The bottom line is this: New birth is known by its fruits, not by a decision. The most important fruit is hunger for God himself (p. 30).

When reading this, I thought, "Yes! A hunger for God is what I'm trying to develop with my girls." I've realized in my own faith journey, that as my hunger for God increased, I begin to read my word, pray, and share God's Word with others. It was this hunger that sparked the seeds of change in my way of thinking, my "renewed mind."

Do not conform to the pattern of this world, but be transformed by the renewing of your mind. Then you will be able to test and approve what God's will is—his good, pleasing and perfect will. (Romans 12:2)

All who have this hope in him purify themselves, just as he is pure. Everyone who sins breaks the law; in fact, sin is lawlessness. But you know that he appeared so that he might take away our sins. And in him is no sin. No one who lives in him keeps on sinning. No one who continues to sin has either seen him or known him. No one who is born of God will continue to sin, because God's seed remains in them; they cannot go on sinning, because they have been born of God. (1 John 3: 3-6, 9)

With this explanation in mind, sanctification or Farley's description of "new birth" may appear in various ways in your girls. You might find them start to be more open to asking questions about God's Word as the group moves along. You might find that their "highs and lows" during the Check-In portion of the session will start to take into account blessings and convictions that come with developing a stronger relationship with Christ. Their attitudes, behaviors, willingness to learn about God, and openness to discuss the joys and struggles of their faith journey may become more transparent and in line with God's word.

To me, the process of sanctification explains both parts of Romans 10:9, which states that our salvation comes from confessing Jesus as Lord with our mouths and also believing in our hearts. The confession is the easy part, but the believing in our hearts (read: changing our behavior, mindset, attitudes to align with our belief that Jesus is Lord and He died for our sins) is often the hardest part. We show our love and our faith to the Father by keeping His commands because we really believe them. Now, this does not mean we are going to get it right all the time, but our intention is to please our Heavenly Father through our representation of Him in the world.

If you declare with your mouth, "Jesus is Lord," and believe in your heart that God raised him from the dead, you will be saved. For it is with your heart that you believe and are justified, and it is with your mouth that you profess your faith and are saved. (Romans 10:9-10)

If you love me, keep my commands. Whoever has my commands and keeps them is the one who loves me. The one who loves me will be loved by my Father, and I too will love them and show myself to them."(John 14: 15, 21)

Sanctification takes time to develop. Their ability to grow in this way is also influenced by the frequency and duration that you work with the girls, as well as their connection to a family and faith community that supports their Christian development. Given this, you may not get to "see" this developing in the girls. While we are planting seeds, it may be another believer's watering down the road that will lead the girls to a personal relationship with God. Don't be discouraged! Take heart and know that you are planting seeds, although the harvest may not come to pass until a later season. We cannot abandon our assignment to share the faith. God will provide the increase in the appropriate season because His word cannot return void.

So neither the one who plants nor the one who waters is anything, but only God, who makes things grow. The one who plants and the one who waters have one purpose, and they will each be rewarded according to their own labor. For we are co-workers in God's service;

you are God's field, God's building. (1 Corinthians 3:7-9)

As the rain and the snow come down from heaven, and do not return to it without watering the earth and making it bud and flourish, so that it yields seed for the sower and bread for the eater, so is my word that goes out from my mouth: It will not return to me empty, but will accomplish what I desire and achieve the purpose for which I sent it. (Isaiah 55:10-11)

Curriculum Format

The Destined D.I.V.A. curriculum is organized around six themes. Each theme has several sessions that expound on each theme. Each session's format is user-friendly and provides a thorough outline with associated icons to lead the group session from start to finish. A suggested script for session activities and discussion are found in italic text, with the statement "share with the group," preceding the italic text. Additionally, focus scriptures are provided to support the group discussions and activities.

The Destined D.I.V.A. sessions are planned to take approximately 1.5 hours to complete in order to accommodate information sharing, group discussion, interactive activities, and prayer. However, feel free to adjust the sessions as necessary to fit within your time constraints. If the group discussion or questions from the girls causes the lesson to extend past your scheduled meeting time, you may continue the lesson the next time

you are scheduled to meet, for a "part two" of the same topic so you can cover everything. This usually works well if the group meets weekly or at another frequent interval. Sessions consists of the following components:

Check-In: Opening ice-breaker to get updates from group members on how they are doing. Check-In provides an opportunity to get group members plugged into the session and to share experiences with the group. There are several options for facilitating Check-In. These include having all girls give their "highs and lows" of the week (see description below), or making up your own activity.

Instructions for "Highs and Lows" Check-In Activity:

"Highs and lows" is a simple discussion activity that I like to use for my D.I.V.A. group. Each girl gives her "high" (good thing) and "low" (not so good thing) that occurred during the past week. Depending on the number of girls present, the Leader may want to limit each girl to having a certain amount of time (i.e. one minute per girl). The group participants may ask questions for clarification, but this time is not intended for group discussion. Instead, it is intended for each girl to share "where she is" at the present time.

If the girls have difficulty with respecting each person's turn, the Leader should reiterate group rules, but may also want to implement a "talking stick" into the Check-In process. A "talking stick" (or whatever the group names it) is a particular item used to indicate who should be allowed to talk at a given time. Usually, only one person can have the "talking stick" at a time. This visual component may help the group to adhere to the group rule of respecting others while they are speaking.

I usually start each session like this, and I've found that it is non-intimidating and gives every girl an opportunity to contribute to the group because it's personal and there are no wrong answers. Additionally, the predictability of a consistent Check-In process adds to the group dynamic, and the girls actually become excited each week to share their personal ups and downs. This part of the session also gives the D.I.V.A. Leader an opportunity to make inferences about possible prayer requests to include in group prayer. The Leader can also identify if there are areas needing follow up with a particular girl; before or after a session for mentoring, or connecting the girl to additional resources as appropriate.

Recall (if applicable): Discuss and refresh key concepts from previous sessions.

How to facilitate the Recall segment:

Ask the group what they remember from the previous session. Review some of the key concepts from the last session. Ask the group if anyone can relate anything from their life to the topic since the last meeting. Discuss any exercises the girls completed in the D.I.V.A. Handbook since the last session. If necessary, review the D.I.V.A. acronym and group rules discussed in session 1.

Foundation: Provides purpose and introduction to the topic and scriptural text for the session

Activity: Creative, interactive learning activity designed to address the topic of the session, reinforce learning concepts, and encourage reflection.

Discussion: Facilitated group discussion to draw out group member's perspectives, and share what was learned or how the scripture and activity can be applied to the girls' lives.

D.I.V.A. Challenge: An action the girls must take during the week to "work out their faith," and try to put session concepts into action.

Closing Reflection and Prayer: Closing takeaway points, exercises done individually or as a group to reflect on our relationship with Christ and to reflect on how the scripture can be applied to our lives through action and prayer.

Although it is not written out for every lesson, it is recommended to offer an opportunity for girls to accept salvation in each session during the closing reflection and prayer time as well, with a reminder that God's promises are for His children that confess their belief in Him. The S.A.Y. It Loud outline explained in Session 21 is a great way to share the components of salvation, while allowing girls to use their own words to respond to the Holy Spirit's drawing. S.A.Y. stands for "see your sin," "accept Jesus," and "you confess it." See Session 21 for a complete description.

Additionally, this would be a good opportunity to invite them to a local church if the group exists outside of a church setting.

Pertinent worksheets for the lesson will immediately follow each session outline and will be available for download by emailing docs@thedestineddivas.com with access code **"DDdocs"** as the subject line.

Multiple Ways You Can Use This Guide

If followed from front to back as is, the curriculum can provide several months of weekly small group sessions to start a Destined D.I.V.A. small group. The Leader's Guide can also be used to complement an already existing small group program where targeted lessons on specific topics may be needed. In this case, the guide can be used to pick and choose specific themes or sessions that are applicable to your group at any given time. The Leader's Guide and the corresponding D.I.V.A. Handbook for teens, are easy to follow, and were developed to be used together. However, both are useful as stand-alone items as well.

Making the Sessions Work in Your Setting

This curriculum is not intended for one-time use. To obtain the maximum benefit, it should be used over time to cultivate understanding and relationships— relationships between the girls, between girls and adult leaders, and most importantly with Christ. Through this type of ongoing interchange, adult group leaders have time to mentor the girls, model biblical principles, and observe growth in group participants. Prayerfully, this guide will enable adult group leaders to further turn a new group into a regular bible-based small group program.

Due to sensitive issues that may arise as participants discuss personal experiences and their successes and challenges on their Christian journey, the following considerations are recommended for optimal group facilitation:

- Dedicated meeting space with a closed door. "Pass-through" meeting spaces that are accessible to individuals not participating in the group, can be distracting and counterproductive to the group dynamic.

- Consistent meeting frequency (i.e. the same day and time on a weekly, biweekly, or monthly basis)

- Group size of 5 – 12 girls to allow for all to participate. However, a larger group may be necessary to involve all interested girls. In this case, it is especially recommended to have an additional group leader.

- Participation with teen girls ages 13-18, as this is the developmental age group this curriculum was developed for.

- Establish group rules in the first session. The girls should take the lead on creating these to help them take ownership of the group. However, the leader should reiterate the rules frequently in the beginning of the group's development, and occasionally revisit them over the life of the group, as the girls become more willing to adhere to the rules. See session one for examples of group rules.

- Maintain the group's confidentiality to build trust with the girls, but also to encourage the "safe space" for the group to grow and learn. Exceptions to this include serious areas of concern involving the safety of the girls or others (i.e. thoughts of suicide, plans to hurt someone else, dangerous romantic relationships, etc.). In these instances, the leader should collaborate with the girl to inform her parents of these concerns. Additional reporting requirements may be required based on the state you are in. Visit www.childwelfare.gov/responding/mandated.cfm to learn about mandated reporting laws for your state. You should also involve your Pastor or appropriate representative from your organization (if applicable) when handling these issues.

Leading the Group

This curriculum is intended to be used by ordinary women that profess to be disciples of Jesus Christ, lovers of God's Word, and seekers of truth. You don't have to be a Bible scholar, perfect, or a "super Christian" to lead this group or mentor girls. The format is user-friendly, and with proper review, preparation, prayer, and a heart for Christ and teen girls...one should be able to lead this. I will state that working with teens and leading a small group is not for everyone. But, the fact that you purchased this book and are reading this right now is an indication that you are a good candidate to lead a Destined D.I.V.A. group!

As it is written: "There is no one righteous, not even one;...for all have sinned and fall short of the glory of God, and all are justified freely by his grace through the redemption that came by Christ Jesus. (Romans 3:10, 23-24)

If you are trying to grow in your own faith, then teen D.I.V.A.s need you! As a D.I.V.A. Leader, one should have a passion for teen girls, be personally seeking the Lord, be making a good faith effort to live according to Christian principles, and be able to model (in word and actions) the lesson aims included in this guide. Visit the "Resources for Destined D.I.V.A. Leaders" section of the website at www.thedestineddivas.com to download the "D.I.V.A. Leader Reflection Worksheet." This worksheet is a self-reflection tool to help you consider your strengths and areas of challenge as a D.I.V.A. Leader. It is highly recommended that you complete the worksheet before you start your Destined D.I.V.A. group.

Additionally, there are some generational considerations to take into account. Although there is no specific age that a leader must be to lead the group, the leader should be approachable and able to relate and respond in a loving way (even if correcting!) to the teen culture. Yes, teens have a specific culture that has its own language, dress, and thought processes! I have found that a "mothering approach" is not as successful in leading this group as a "big sister" approach. This is because the group offers a separate space outside of the parent-child relationship for girls to be taught, encouraged, and redirected in the way of Christ. Oftentimes, teens may not be completely honest with their parents for a variety of reasons, with 'not wanting to disappoint them' being one of the major ones. The "big sister" approach eliminates some of these relationship dynamics, and has been most effective at discipling girls to Christ in this context.

Here are some tips for effectively leading the group:

- Review the session thoroughly before leading it, so you will be familiar and comfortable with the content. This will allow you to spend more of your time connecting with the girls in the teaching and sharing process of the session rather than focusing on "following the curriculum."

- Start with Session One to set the tone of the group and create group rules.

It is recommended that you follow up with the sessions in the first module, It's a Two Way Street, regardless of whether or not you use the lessons in order in the rest of the book. The sessions in this module introduce the spiritual framework for receiving salvation and establishing a personal relationship with God. This framework lays the groundwork for the life skills discussed in later parts of the book.

- PRAY! Pray before and after the sessions and pray for the girls during the week, that they will be able to implement the concepts from the curriculum into their daily lives.

- Try to live the things you are teaching. It will make your instruction and mentoring for the girls so much more powerful to help lead them in the way of Christ.

- Give thanks for the seeds you are planting in the girls, even if you cannot readily see if any of the biblical principles are taking root in them.

- Find other women to take this journey with you, so that doing this alone will not be overwhelming. Encouragement and accountability are very important to all involved in this process!

- Keep in mind that it may take some time for connections between the girls in the group to develop, especially if the girls did not know each other before attending the group. Groups go through a lot of stages, so it may take some time for everyone to gel and take ownership of the group.

- Make this curriculum your own. Although I have attempted to provide a layout that is easy to follow and encourages women to step into this leadership role, it is your personality, love, energy, and enthusiasm combined with God's word that will make this information come ALIVE for the girls!

About Teen Development

The Destined D.I.V.A. curriculum takes a positive youth development approach, a strength-based model that takes into account the capacities, strengths, and developmental needs of youth. The aim is to facilitate and support young people's growth through dependence to interdependence (National Youth Agency Statement of Principles UK, December 2001). This view assumes that teens have a lot of potential and ability to do great things for God's kingdom while they are still teens, and that as adults, it is our job to give them the tools to help them to do it. Empowering young people is the work of youth development.

The teen years are an especially tumultuous time of development, as young people are on the cusp of adulthood. In some instances they are already treated as adults. And although cognitively they are more and more sophisticated at problem-solving and processing the situations in their life, emotionally their maturity is still developing and they are still learning to cope with all that life is tossing at them. "The early adolescence state of development (12-18 years) begins with the onset of puberty and ends with the graduation from high school. This stage of development is characterized by rapid physical changes, significant cognitive and emotional maturation, newly energized sexual interests, and a heightened sensitivity to peer relations" *(Newman, B. and Newman, P. 2008, Development through Life: A Psychosocial Approach. Cengage Learning, p. 318).*

Keep these developmental tasks that are taking place in this stage in mind when working with the girls:

- Self-identity becomes stronger through articulation of ideas, values, and plans for the future

- Thinking ahead and establishing realistic future plans are important to help make informed and reasoned decisions

- Formulating "right and wrong" ideas and how to act on them with less adult guidance

- Peer to peer discussions regarding experiences, norms, behaviors, and consequences increase

- Identifying some situations as "unfair" or "hypocritical" begins

- Feelings of anxiety and self-consciousness about physical development and growth increase

- New experiences create a range of new emotions

- Learning coping mechanisms to handle new experiences increase

- Seeking personal advice from adults and finding new social resources for support is challenging

- Seeking greater autonomy, but not complete independence; testing and questioning limits with adults

- Peer conflict between "wanting to fit in" with peers and "standing up for what is right"

- Confidence in social skills and understanding of social expectations strengthens

As you can see, our girls are navigating through a LOT of changes at this time in their life. Mentoring by women at this critical time can help them choose the path towards Christ. The D.I.V.A. curriculum integrates scripture, mentoring, and life skill development to help address all of these areas from a spiritual perspective.

Ideas to Increase Accountability

Again, our goal is to plant seeds so sanctification in Christ can develop in the girls. As part of the discipleship process, repetition and reinforcement of learning concepts is very important. Additionally, accountability to each other is a pillar of the Christian faith.

As iron sharpens iron, so one person sharpens another. (Proverbs 27:17)

Here are some tips that I have found that help to keep the girls engaged, and to increase accountability between group sessions:

Provide Bibles and Destined D.I.V.A. Handbooks for the girls

Some girls will have their own Bibles; others may be just getting involved with the Christian faith. One purpose of this group is to empower girls to develop their own personal relationship with Christ. Knowing how to use the Bible, and learning about the necessity of reading the Bible is critical to this purpose being fulfilled. I recommend a user-friendly translation that will be easier for the girls to understand, such as the New Living Translation or The Message.

Additionally, adding journaling activities is a great way to facilitate personal reflection among the girls between sessions. These handbook prompts are built into The Destined D.I.V.A. Handbook, a companion product to this curriculum.

Obtaining Bibles and handbooks for all the girls in your group can be expensive, so check with your church or organization for funds available, or organize a fundraiser that the girls can lead to raise funds for Bibles and special events. You can use the donation letter template in the FORMS section to collect donations to use towards these costs. I received most of my funds for Bibles, handbooks, and special events for my D.I.V.A. group from donations (cash and the actual items) from Christian women in my church that were supportive of the group, as well as special collections taken up by my Pastor for youth outreach.

Use Social Media to Reinforce Learning

Social media permeates our society. With the emergence of less desirable activities like cyber-bullying and sexting, social media can be re-purposed for Kingdom-building and to counter these negative activities.

- Develop a Facebook page for your group that can only be accessed by the members in it. Scriptures, journal prompts, in-between-session check-ins, and D.I.V.A. Challenges can be posted as a reminder here. It's especially effective to have this managed by one (or two) of the girls from the group.

- Develop a Twitter profile so the girls (and everyone else!) can "follow" you as you post tweets that are reminders or encouragement to "live out" session goals during the week.

- Develop a text message list for sending reminders throughout the week.

Implement an Incentive System

When leading my group, I found that there were times when the girls were not taking the challenges, reading their Bibles, or journaling throughout the week. I came up with the D.I.V.A. Dollar incentive system to encourage them to do these activities throughout the week (See template in FORMS section of the book). As part of the RECALL section of the session, we would review the previous week's session including journal prompts, focus scriptures, and weekly challenges. Any girls that did any of these activities received a D.I.V.A. Dollar, which could be used for raffles. Raffle prizes can be anything, such as inexpensive items from the local dollar store, donated items, or a group reward to encourage accountability between the girls (i.e. when each girl has acquired 8 D.I.V.A. Dollars, the group will get a pizza party). I have found the incentive system to be very effective.

Now, I know some will say, "We don't want to bribe the girls to read their Bibles!" I agree 100%, but I don't think of this as a bribe. Just as we can get an extra bonus for doing good work at our jobs, something we are supposed to do anyway, getting recognized for it is quite an encouragement to keep doing good work! Additionally, we are trying to encourage "new birth," and when that occurs, the girls will read their Bibles because they will want to and see the necessity of it for their lives. I think of the incentive system as one way to help them get into God's Word, so He can manifest the transforming power of the Word in their lives.

Plan Social Outings and Events

Fellowship is essential to the Christian faith, and it encourages relationship-building between group members and adult leaders. Given the importance placed on peer relationships in this developmental stage, opportunities for social interactions among Christian youth is very important to their spiritual development. Again, there will be costs incurred here, so tap into those donation and fundraising ideas mentioned earlier. In addition, the girls may have to chip in for outing costs as well. See FORMS section in the back of the book for templates for parent permission slip/transportation releases. Here are some fellowship ideas:

- Attending local youth expos and conferences to fellowship with other youth in the area

- Community service projects to encourage the servant leadership modeled by Jesus Christ

- Miscellaneous fellowship outings – sports events, plays, skating, bowling, water parks, amusement parks, etc.

- D.I.V.A. Overnight Retreat

- Recognition luncheon to acknowledge individual strides and growth of group members of an established D.I.V.A. group. Invite parents, church members, and others to celebrate the girls' accomplishments in the group

- Destined D.I.V.A. open houses to introduce the group in a new setting, invite new members to an established group, or to re-engage with girls that have discontinued attending the group

READY, SET, GO!

With some of the elements I mentioned above, there are so many opportunities to grow and expand this group in your church, family, or organization. Perhaps Destined D.I.V.A. can be an ongoing small group Bible study, or it can become a full-fledged ministry in your church under the overall youth and/or women's ministry umbrellas. This has been the case at my church, and it has been such a blessing to me, the girls, and the congregation as a whole.

Remember, one plants the seed and another may water it. Every effort that is made from parenting, to engagement in the local church, to individual mentoring relationships, to the Destined D.I.V.A. group you are about to lead, is helping to prepare our girls for their futures.

Most importantly, these efforts are bringing them closer to Christ. Congratulations to you for having the desire to encourage and support teen girls. May God bless you richly and add the increase to your life! Use the D.I.V.A. outreach card and letter to parents (in the FORMS section in the back of the book) to spread the word about this fun, awesome, and life-changing group you are about to start. Now, let's get to discipling some D.I.V.A.s!

In Christ,
Laura E. Knights, MSW

Session 1

Laying the Foundation

SESSION GOALS:

D.I.V.A. participants will:

- Introduce themselves and get to know each other
- Establish rules to govern the group sessions
- Understand the purpose of the group, and understand that the group lessons will build upon their faith in God
- Review the Destined D.I.V.A. acronym, and commit to participating in the group

SCRIPTURE FOCUS:

Hebrews 11:1 & 6 (NLT); Romans 10:17

MATERIALS NEEDED:

- D.I.V.A. Handbooks, one book for each girl
- Bibles: Inform the girls to bring Bibles if they have them
- Roster template (See FORMS section)
- Name tags (if needed)
- D.I.V.A. acronym sheet
- Individually wrapped multicolored candy such as Star Bursts or Jolly

- Ranchers; you will need at least three different colors/flavors and enough for each girl to have at least one piece
- Flip chart paper and markers

PREP TASKS:

Copy the D.I.V.A. acronym sheet for girls that do not have a D.I.V.A. Handbook; or make a poster with the acronym displayed.

GETTING STARTED

Explain that today's session will be an introduction to the Destined D.I.V.A. group and an opportunity for everyone to get to know each other. Introduce yourself to the group as the D.I.V.A. Leader that will be facilitating the group.

CHECK –IN

Pass around D.I.V.A. roster for each girl to sign in. Have the girls introduce themselves and complete name tags if needed. Distribute a D.I.V.A. Handbook to each girl.

ACTIVITY: Candy Choices Partner Up

1. Count the girls off by two or instruct them to partner up with someone they don't know well
2. Let the girls pick one piece of candy, but do not tell them that the candy colors have meaning
3. Instruct the girls to share their name, what they hope to get out of participating in the group, and the response to the following candy choice questions based on the color/flavor they picked.

   -Candy Color A – If you could have any supernatural power, what would it be?
   -Candy Color B – If you could change anything about your life, what would it be?
   -Candy Color C – If you could change anything from the past, what would it be?

4. After both partners have shared, bring the girls back to the large group. Each girl presents her partner and their answers to the questions to the group.

FOUNDATION

Share with the group:

The purpose of this Destined D.I.V.A. group is to help you to navigate issues you may be dealing within your life and to help you grow in your personal relationship with God. The hope is that you will grow closer to God and each other through learning more scripture and understand how it applies to your life, and by growing closer to the girls and the leader of the group. We will share real life situations, share in group discussions, and do fun activities to help us learn the lessons in each session.

Ask the girls, "What do you think it means to be a Destined D.I.V.A.?" and solicit their responses.

Review the Destined D.I.V.A. acronym using the sheet provided after this lesson. Ask the girls to share their thoughts on the acronym. Ask the group to commit to displaying these traits moving forward. Inform them that you will review the acronym over the duration of your group.

Provide the topics you will be covering in the group over the next few sessions to give the girls some idea of what will be discussed in the group. You may want to give them the opportunity to choose some sessions they would like to cover sooner rather than later to allow them to have some input.

If you will expand the group to have occasional social outings/field trips outside of meeting for the sessions, this would be a good time to discuss this as well.

Explain that the D.I.V.A. Handbook will allow the girls to reflect on the lesson topics in between sessions, and that they should bring it with their Bibles to each group session.

ACTIVITY: Creating Group Rules

Share with the group:

This group is a safe space for everyone to share. We must show love in this group. As a group, we will develop group rules that we all must commit to following. It is our job to make sure that we respect the rules that we create for the group to be successful and for everyone to enjoy participating in it. We cannot feel comfortable to share and grow if anyone feels that they cannot be themselves in this group. Nothing is off limits to discuss in this group.

Attach flip chart paper to the wall. Ask for a volunteer to write the rules on the paper using the markers. Lead the group in brainstorming appropriate rules for the group. Instruct the volunteer to write down all ideas, and the group can edit the list after the brainstorming is completed. Suggested rules include, but are not limited to:

- Don't judge people
- Confidentiality within the group
- Everyone has an opportunity to speak
- Encourage each other – no put downs
- Respect each other – don't interrupt when others are speaking
- Participate – we can learn from everyone here
- Tech-free zone – turn off cell phones, IPods, and other devices while in session

Inform the girls that rules will be posted and reviewed prior to the start of each session moving forward.

DISCUSSION

Ask the girls to rate the strength of their personal relationship with God, with 1 being "weak" and 10 being "strong." Go around the group and allow each person to share. Inform the girls that the group is about growing, and that it's okay to be honest because this group will help them to build their faith and grow in their relationship with God.

Ask the girls to share their definitions and thoughts on faith.

Share with the group:

Throughout our time in this group, we will talk about the importance of having faith because our faith sets the foundation for everything we will do in this group.

Ask everyone to stand up and sit back down on their chairs. Make an observation that everyone (or most people) stood up and sat back down without turning around to look at the chair. Ask the girls why they didn't need to look back at their chair before sitting back down. You may receive responses like, "I knew it was there" or "I was just sitting on it."

Ask someone to read Hebrews 11:1 & 6(NLT)

Faith is the confidence that what we hope for will actually happen; it gives us assurance about things we cannot see.And it is impossible to please God without faith. Anyone who wants to come to him must believe that God exists and that he rewards those who sincerely seek him.

Share with the group:

This is how our faith in God works. We cannot always see him, but we have to trust and have confidence that He is there. We cannot please God or grow in our relationship with Him if we don't have faith. There will be times in your life, when you know that the only way you made it out of a particular situation or felt better about something bad that happened is because you knew that God was there guiding and protecting you.

Ask if anyone has an example of one of these situations from their own life.

Ask if anyone in the group would like more faith. Connect this need for more faith back to the 1-10 rating responses they gave on their personal relationship with God.

Ask the group how do you get more faith and discuss their responses.

Ask someone to read Romans 10:17

Consequently, faith comes from hearing the message, and the message is heard through the word about Christ.

Share with the group:

As children of God, our salvation is based on our faith. Having salvation means that you accept Jesus as your savior, and because of his death on the cross and resurrection, you are free from the power of sin over your life. We will learn more about salvation in a future lesson. Our faith determines our strength and courage to make it through life's challenges. Our faith affects our choices and decisions. Our faith is fueled by the Word of God, and as we learn more about Him through His Word, we grow in our faith.

Ask the girls if they can relate to this in their own lives. Ask them if they can share examples, either from their life or someone else's, when faith affected actions:

- Faith affecting one's courage (For example, someone did something that was difficult or scary for them to do because they felt like God would see them through it; or conversely, they did not do it because they felt God was not with them)
- Faith affecting one's choices and decisions

D.I.V.A. CHALLENGE

Share with the group:

The D.I.V.A. Challenge for this week is for everyone to read Romans 12 and to attempt to pray at least three times this week. (Increase or decrease the prayer time as appropriate for your group.)

Write about it in your handbook.

Tell the girls you will ask them to report on their progress with this challenge at the next session.

CLOSING REFLECTION & PRAYER

Share with the group:

We have discussed the purpose of our Destined D.I.V.A. group and some of the topics we will cover together. We have also discussed that our faith is a very important part of our personal relationship with God. As we begin to have more sessions together, think about the areas in your life where you need more faith. Pray about these areas in your private time with God throughout the week. Remember, this is your group. You will get out of it what you put into it.

Invite a girl to pray out loud for the group based on the topic discussed. End the session with this prayer:

Father, thank you for the young women in this group that have a desire to grow closer to you. Draw them closer to you to help them increase their faith. Place a yearning in them to learn your Word and to become more aware of your presence in their lives. Help us to commit to the rules so that this group is a safe space for everyone that wants to be a part of it. Use this group for your glory.

Destined – ordained, appointed, or predetermined to be or do something

Daughters – of Christ and wonderfully beheld in His eyes

Integrity – Complete, undivided, and adhering to Christian values; committed to letting our words match our actions

Virtue – Full of beautiful attributes and having the power to put them into action

IT'S A TWO WAY STREET
Sessions 2-5

Theme Overview:

The sessions in this theme center on the single most important relationship one could ever have—a personal relationship with God. These sessions focus on understanding salvation, understanding the consequences of continued sin, learning how to pray, and embracing a new identity as a child of God. The girls will learn that, just like in any other relationship, building a relationship with their Heavenly Father is a "two-way street." God demonstrates His love for us in so many ways, but there are also some requirements He asks of us to grow closer and develop a personal relationship with Him.

Session 2

Extreme Makeover

SESSION GOALS:

D.I.V.A. participants will:
- Understand that our sinful nature is why we need Jesus Christ
- Discuss how sin separates us from God
- Understand God's grace and mercy towards us that is offered through Jesus Christ

SCRIPTURE FOCUS:

John 3:16; Romans 5:6-8 (NLT); Romans 6:23; Romans 10:9; Romans 3:10, 23-24; Ephesians 2:8-9 (NLT); John 14:15-17, 26

See also Genesis 1-3, John 19 & 20

MATERIALS NEEDED:

- D.I.V.A. Handbooks, one book for each girl
- Bibles: Inform the girls to bring Bibles if they have them
- Salvation Illustration Handout
- Extreme Makeover Activity Worksheet Color pencils/markers
- Flip chart paper

PREP TASKS:

- Recreate the salvation illustration on the flip chart paper and post so everyone can see it
- Make a copy of the Extreme Makeover Activity Worksheets

CHECK –IN

Make up your own Check-In activity or facilitate the "Highs and Lows" Check-In activity described in the introduction on page 17.

FOUNDATION:

Share with the group:

Today we are talking about salvation and being a follower of Christ. Some people call this "being saved." Many young people call themselves Christians because their parents are Christian or because they go to church, but those things do not make you a Christian or "saved." Many teens say that they will wait until they grow up to get serious about God. The truth of the matter is that we hear about young people dying every day on the news and in our communities. We do not know how long we have on this earth, and heaven and hell are real! God wants us to make a decision to follow Him NOW, and not only because He wants you with Him in heaven, but because He wants you to experience His love right now on earth too. The goal is not to scare you into believing in Him, but it is for you to understand His love and for you to CHOOSE to live your life for Him. It is a very personal decision. Your parents and your friends cannot make the decision for you. Today we will learn how we can be saved.

Lead the group in a brief discussion using the following prompts:

- How many have accepted Jesus Christ as their Lord and Savior and are "saved"?
- For those that say yes:
  - In your own words, what does it mean to be saved?
  - What made you choose to accept Him?
  - How do you know you are saved?

Ask someone to read the following scriptures:

John 3:16
For God so loved the world that he gave his one and only Son, that whoever believes in him shall not perish but have eternal life.

Romans 5:6-8 (NLT)
When we were utterly helpless, Christ came at just the right time and died for us sinners. Now, most people would not be willing to die for an upright person, **though someone might perhaps be willing to die for a person who is especially good. But God showed his great love for us by sending Christ to die for us while we were still sinners.**

Romans 6:23
For the wages of sin is death, but the gift of God is eternal life in Christ Jesus our Lord.

Romans 10:9
If you declare with your mouth, "Jesus is Lord," and believe in your heart that God raised him from the dead, you will be saved.

Refer to the illustration and scriptures just read, and use these points to help explain it:

Our Problem

When God created the first man and woman, Adam and Eve, he gave them specific instructions of what to do and what not to do. They disobeyed God, which created sin. (Tell them they can read about this in Genesis 1-3). Since we all come from Adam and Eve, we inherited that sin. We were born in it. Because God is so holy, he cannot be in the presence of sin. So when Adam sinned, and when we sin, God removes His presence from us. This is death. Not a physical death, but a spiritual death. A spiritual death is separation from God, which creates a huge gap between us and God. We would have no communication or relationship with Him. Apart from God is a dangerous place to be!

God's Solution

Because God loved us so much, He does not want us to be separate from Him. He sent his only Son Jesus who He loved so much to come stand in the gap between us. We deserved to take the consequences for our sin. This includes suffering while we are on Earth, and going to hell when we die for our sin. But Jesus came down from heaven and suffered a horrible death for us. He was killed and buried.

Three days after his burial, God brought Him back to life and He had all the power in His hands. Forty days after his resurrection, He went back to heaven to be with God. He had completed His assignment. He took our place and saved us from having to suffer the horrible consequences of our sin. When he died that one time, He took our death penalty for EVERY sin we would ever commit. This is why we call Him Savior (Tell them they can read about it in John 19 & 20).

Our Response

Salvation is our first opportunity for life with God. To receive this gift, we acknowledge the huge sacrifice Jesus made by accepting him as our Savior. We say it out of our mouths that we believe He died and was brought back life for us. Then after we say that, we show that we really believe it in our hearts by turning away from sin. This means we give everything we have to in order to do what God tells us to do in His Word, and we stop doing the things that He says is not good for us. We then take advantage of our renewed relationship with God by praising and thanking Him every day,

praying, reading the Bible so we can know what He wants for us to do, and loving and serving others. This is what it means by giving your life to God.

Ask the group, if they understand the illustration. Ask them for the questions they still have about salvation? If you cannot answer them, write them down so you can study to find the answers or talk with your pastor/minister to bring back answers to the group at a later time.

Ask someone to read the following scriptures:

Romans 3:10, 23-24
As it is written: "There is no one righteous, not even one;...for all have sinned and fall short of the glory of God, and all are justified freely by his grace through the redemption that came by Christ Jesus.

Ephesians 2:8-9 (NLT)
God saved you by his grace when you believed. And you can't take credit for this; it is a gift from God. Salvation is not a reward for the good things we have done, so none of us can boast about it.

Share with the group:

There is nothing we could do to deserve salvation. It is a gift from God, given to us because He loves us. Everyone makes mistakes and everyone has sin inside of them, this is why we need Jesus. When you accept Him and do these things, He will come into your heart and begin to change you. You will begin to look like Him in the way you talk, act, and think about things. You will have a different view on life. God changing you from the inside out is evidence of being saved. He performs an extreme makeover on us! This is what it means to be "born again."

ACTIVITY: Extreme Makeover

Distribute the Extreme Makeover Activity Worksheets and colored pencils. Ask the group to think about areas in their life where they need an extreme makeover. Ask everyone to complete the exercise individually, and then share with a partner to discuss any similarities. Then, have the group come back to the large group so everyone can share their responses.

DISCUSSION:

Based on the activity, lead the girls in a discussion using the following prompts:
- Share the areas where you need an extreme makeover?
- Why do you believe you need an extreme makeover in this area?
- What specifically do you need God to do for you?

Share with the group:

These are a lot of big changes that you all want to make! How do you think we will accomplish these things? Discuss their responses.

Ask someone to read John 14:15-17, 26

If you love me, keep my commands. And I will ask the Father, and he will give you another advocate to help you and be with you forever— the Spirit of truth. The world cannot accept him, because it neither sees him nor knows him. But you know him, for he lives with you and will be in you. But the Advocate, the Holy Spirit, whom the Father will send in my name, will teach you all things and will remind you of everything I have said to you.

Share with the group:

Once we accept Jesus as our Lord and Savior, He gives us his spirit--the Holy Spirit-- to live inside of us. The Holy Spirit represents God's love. The Holy Spirit leads us and helps us to make decisions as we are being changed by Christ. From the scripture we just heard, we see that Jesus asks us to do something too. He says "If you love me, keep my commands." Then, Jesus will go to God on your behalf, so that He will give you the Holy Spirit. You see, it's a two way street! We have to give something—our life —to get the rewards of God!

D.I.V.A. CHALLENGE:

Share with the group:

The D.I.V.A. Challenge for this week is to re-read the scriptures from this session.

Write about it in your handbook.

Tell the girls you will ask them to report on their progress with this challenge at the next session.

CLOSING REFLECTION AND PRAYER:

Ask the girls if anyone would like to accept Jesus Christ as their Lord and Savior. If so, review the key points of salvation using the S.A.Y. Outline (See Session 21 for more details), and encourage the girls to say their own prayer of salvation. Help them if they are having difficulty, but allow them to come up with their own words.

The S.A.Y. Outline:

S - "See your sin." We all have sinned. No one is perfect.

A - "Accept Jesus." Accept that Jesus Christ is God's Son. Willingly accept Jesus' gift of forgiveness from sin.

Y - "You confess it." Confess your faith in Jesus Christ as Savior and Lord with your mouth.

End the session with this prayer:

Father, thank you for this opportunity to share your Word and the message of salvation. I pray that your Word will touch our hearts, and lead us to grow closer to you. If there are girls here who have not accepted you as their Lord and Savior, I pray that they may have a personal experience with you that may lead them to accept you as their Lord and Savior. I pray that the seeds planted today will yield beautiful disciples for your Kingdom. In Jesus name we pray. Amen.

Session 2 Handout: Salvation Illustration

GOD

US

GOD'S REMEDY

JESUS

Romans 5:8

1 Peter 3:18

OUR PROBLEM

Sin
Romans 3:23

Death
Romans 6:23

OUR RESPONSE

Believe & Confess
Romans 10:9-10

Repent & Baptism
Acts 2:38

RESULTS IN

Eternal life
No judgment
Death to life
John 5: 24

Session 2 Worksheet: Extreme Makeover

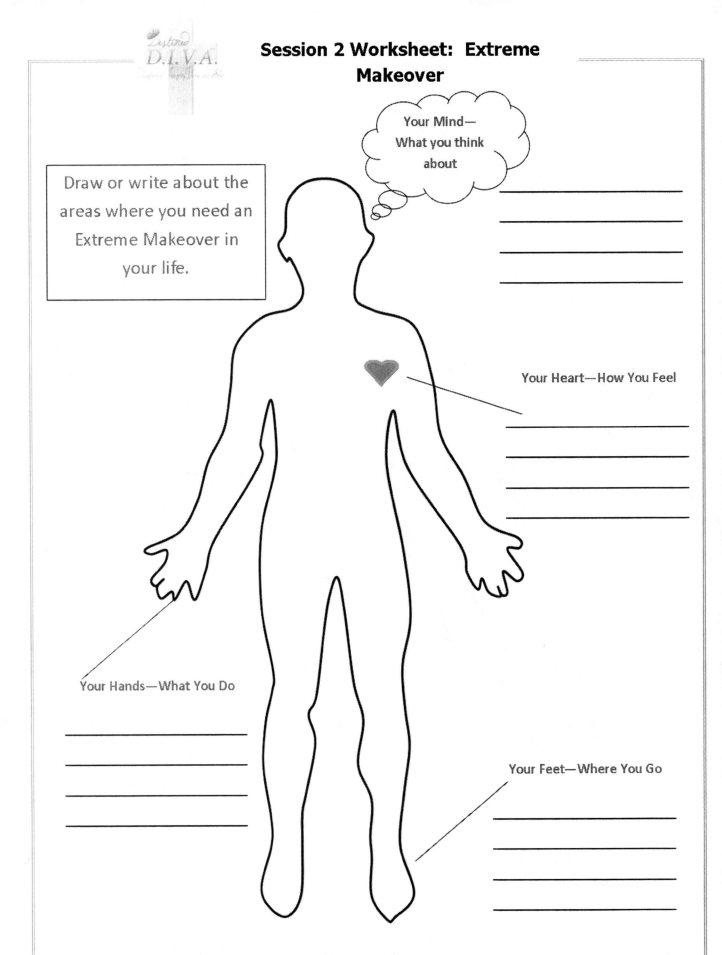

Draw or write about the areas where you need an Extreme Makeover in your life.

Your Mind—What you think about

Your Heart—How You Feel

Your Hands—What You Do

Your Feet—Where You Go

Session 3

Hardheaded Ways

SESSION GOALS:

D.I.V.A. participants will:
- Understand that sin has consequences that can negatively affect our lives and the lives of others
- Understand that true repentance – asking for forgiveness AND turning away from the sin—is needed to please God
- Understand that God is faithful to forgive us because we have victory over sin through Jesus Christ

SCRIPTURE FOCUS:

Romans 3:22-24 (NLT); Psalm 51:5; Mark 7:20-23 (The Message); James 1:13-15 (NLT); Romans 6:23; Romans 7:15-20 (NLT); 2Timothy 2:22; 1 John 1: 9; 1 Corinthians 15:57; Romans 8:1-3b

MATERIALS NEEDED:
- D.I.V.A. Handbooks, one book for each girl
- Bibles: Inform the girls to bring Bibles if they have them
- 2-3 Spools of Yarn
- Several pair of scissors

PREP TASKS:
- Divide the yarn into pieces measuring three yards in length; prepare enough pieces for half of the group

RECALL (if applicable)

If applicable, follow the directions for facilitating the recall segment described in the introduction on page 18.

CHECK –IN:

Make up your own Check-In activity or facilitate the "Highs and Lows" Check-In activity described in the introduction on page 17

FOUNDATION

Ask someone to read Romans 3:22-24(NLT)

We are made right with God by placing our faith in Jesus Christ. And this is true for everyone who believes, no matter who we are. For everyone has sinned; we all fall short of God's glorious standard. Yet God, with undeserved kindness,

declares that we are righteous. He did this through Christ Jesus when he freed us from the penalty for our sins.

Share with the group:

The Bible tells us that everyone will sin and fall short of God's glory. This is why we needed Jesus to die for us—to save us from the sin that would separate us from God. Sin when continued asking for forgiveness and turning away from those behaviors has major consequences that not only affect us, but those around us as well. This will be our topic today.

Ask the group, "What comes to mind when you hear about sin?" Allow the girls to share and encourage them to name things that they think are sins.

Share with the group:

There is no easy way to define sin. There are no big or little sins. All sin begins to build walls between us and God. Sin is anything that goes against God's word or plan for your life. Sometimes we sin and we aren't aware of it. Other times, we are fully aware that our actions, behaviors, and thoughts are not pleasing to God. Everyone struggles with sin. This is why Jesus Christ died for us —to take the punishment for us for our sin and bring us back into a beautiful relationship with our Heavenly Father. For the purpose of our lesson today, we will focus on areas that we know are sins that are hard for us to turn away from.

Select some girls to read the following scriptures, and share the comments between scriptures:

Psalm 51:5
Surely I was sinful at birth, sinful from the time my mother conceived me.

Mark 7:20-23 (MSG)
He went on: "It's what comes out of a person that pollutes: obscenities, lusts, thefts, murders, adulteries, greed, depravity, deceptive dealings, carousing, mean looks, slander, arrogance, foolishness—all these are vomit from the heart. There is the source of your pollution."

Human beings are born into sin. From when we are little, we will have the temptation to do things that we know we are not supposed to do…think about it. People always say, "The devil made me do it." Yes, the devil is real, but we have a choice too. Many times our sinful ways come from what we WANT to do, not what we are being forced to do. Because we all will sin, there is no way to completely avoid it. However, as we grow more aware of God's Word by reading our Bible, spending time in prayer, and participating in activities like church, Bible study, D.I.V.A. group, we become more in tune with God's plan for our life.

James 4:17
If anyone, then, knows the good they ought to do and doesn't do it, it is sin for them.

There are some behaviors that the Bible clearly states are wrong for everyone to do (i.e. killing, stealing, lying, etc.). However, this walk with God is personal. There are some things God will hold you accountable for, that won't be wrong for someone else to do. The difference is knowledge!

Sometimes you are not aware that your actions aren't pleasing to God, but once you know better, you have to do better. You will have to 'fess up' to God for your own actions, not the actions of others.

James 1:13-15 (NLT)
And remember, when you are being tempted, do not say, "God is tempting me." God is never tempted to do wrong, and he never tempts anyone else. Temptation comes from our own desires, which entice us and drag us away. These desires give birth to sinful actions. And when sin is allowed to grow, it gives birth to death.

Romans 6:23
For the wages of sin is death, but the gift of God is eternal life in Christ Jesus our Lord.

(Refer back to the illustration about salvation in session 2). *Remember in the illustration, sin which leads to death, is what was separating us from God. Death can be an actual death or spiritual death (separation from God). Jesus formed a bridge over death when he gave his life for us. We have a choice; God nor the devil, will force us to do anything. We either hold out or give in to our temptations. God calls us to repent from our sins to be made right with Him. Repent means to ask for forgiveness AND stop doing the sinful action. Many times we ask for forgiveness, but we return to doing the same thing over and over. This causes us to move farther away from God, and it puts us in danger to suffer the consequences of our hard-headed ways!*

Ask the group, "Why do you think God wants us to repent and turn away from sin?"

Allow the girls to share their thoughts on the question.

ACTIVITY: All Tied Up

Divide the group into pairs. Instruct the girls that one person in the pair represents a child of God and the other person will represent sin; have them decide what each girl will represent in the pairs. Give the girls representing sin approximately three yards of yarn. Instruct the girls with the yarn to begin to wrap the yarn around their partners' hands (about 20-30 times). Instruct them to wrap it closely, but not so tight that it hurts partner.

As the girls are wrapping the yarn around their partners' hands, tell the girls to shout out areas that they struggle with sin (or areas that most teen girls struggle with if they are not comfortable to personalize the activity). Refer to the yarn and explain that this is how sin works in our lives.

Share with the group:

At first it doesn't seem like it will be much to get out of the sinful behavior, but little by little it traps us until we become stuck in negative lifestyle choices, consequences, and attitudes that keep us doing the sinful behavior.

Ask the girls with their hands tied up to try to break out of the yarn without using a knife or scissors. It will be virtually impossible. Instruct the partner to grab their partners' hands that are tied up and pull them around the room. It will be difficult for the partner to resist with both hands tied up. Yell out some of the sins that the girls shared just a few minutes ago, stating that sometimes it's hard to resist.

Share with the group:

This represents the powerful pull sin has on us, and in several places in God's Word, we are instructed to flee from sin. The very things that we know we are not suppose to do, sometimes become the things we want to do the most. That's why God instructs us to flee. Sometimes we will not have the strength to resist because we want to do that sin so bad. Flee literally means to run away! Our own temptations and desires are so powerful, that we will have to flee from them to resist them.

Read Romans 7:15-20 (NLT)

I don't really understand myself, for I want to do what is right, but I don't do it. Instead, I do what I hate. But if I know that what I am doing is wrong, this shows that I agree that the law is good. So I am not the one doing wrong; it is sin living in me that does it. And I know that nothing good lives in me, that is, in my sinful nature. I want to do what is right, but I can't. I want to do what is good, but I don't. I don't want to do what is wrong, but I do it anyway. But if I do what I don't want to do, I am not really the one doing wrong; it is sin living in me that does it.

Read 2 Timothy 2:22

Flee the evil desires of youth and pursue righteousness, faith, love and peace,

along with those who call on the Lord out of a pure heart.

Share with the group:

Sometimes you may think a "little" sin (such as lying to your mom about where you are after school) is no big deal, but if we do this activity with a thin piece of thread to represent a "little sin" or a thick braided rope to represent a "big sin," the fact remains that we would still be stuck and unable to break free without assistance. The point is that sin is sin, and continuing to engage in behaviors that are against God's Word or plan for our life will leave us trapped and begin to pull us away from God.

Ask the group, "So how do we get out of this mess we've created for ourselves?" Get a few responses from the group.

Share with the group:

Jesus Christ died for our sins so we could have victory over sin. We cannot break free without God's grace. When we confess our sins and truly try to turn away from them, God will forgive us, clean us up, and give us another chance to try to get it right.

Ask someone to read 1 John 1:9

If we confess our sins, he is faithful and just and will forgive us our sins and purify us from all unrighteousness.

Distribute the scissors and tell the girls to cut the yarn to free their partners' hands.

Share with the group:

This represents God's grace, and how he can set us free from sin when we ask for forgiveness. We have the victory over sin! As we strengthen our faith by reading our Word, praying, and learning more about Him, we become stronger and stronger to resist sin and follow God's Word. God does not pronounce us as guilty because when we accept Jesus Christ as our Lord and Savior, we are covered by His blood. When God looks at us, he sees the blood of Jesus Christ covering us, and we are granted mercy for our sins.

Ask girls to read these scriptures:

1 Corinthians 15:57
But thank God! He gives us victory over sin and death through our Lord Jesus Christ.

Romans 8:1-3b
Therefore, there is now no condemnation for those who are in Christ Jesus, because through Christ Jesus the law of the Spirit who gives life has set you free from the law of sin and death. For what the law was powerless to do because it was weakened by the flesh, God did by sending his own Son in the likeness of sinful flesh to be a sin offering.

DISCUSSION

Based on the activity, lead the girls in a discussion using the following prompts:

- What sin is tying you up? What are some behaviors and thoughts that you struggle with that you know are not pleasing to God?
- What is the string that's tying it up? What causes you to want to do this?
- Which area of your life is most affected by this bondage? Do you see an effect on others? Are your relationships strained by this (i.e. with parents, friends, etc.)?
- Could you identify with any of the scriptures we read today?

D.I.V.A. CHALLENGE

Share with the group:

The D.I.V.A. Challenge for this session has three parts: 1.) To consciously pray about the sin that is tying them up throughout the next week; 2.) Get an accountability partner (preferably someone from the group); and 3.) Re-read and reflect on at least two of the scriptures from this session. Write about it in your handbook.

Explain that an accountability partner is someone who they will be honest with about their behaviors and thoughts regarding areas of temptation, and a prayer partner that will help them stay on track. They should speak with the person regularly on an ongoing basis.

CLOSING REFLECTION & PRAYER

Share with the group:

The temptation to sin is at every corner of our lives. Only a relationship with Jesus Christ can help us to become stronger each day to run away from these temptations. Jesus made us winners over our sin when He died for us.

Invite a girl to pray out loud for the group based on the topic discussed. End the session with this prayer:

Father, forgive us when we do wrong, and help us to ask for forgiveness and turn away from anything that does not allow us to shine our light for you. Help us to become aware of what is and what is not pleasing to you as we read your Word more and grow closer to you through prayer and spending time with others that believe in you. Help us to practice wisdom to move away from the people, actions, and desires that tempt us to behave outside of what you want us to do. Thank you for helping us to become more and more aware of your love for us. Thank you for Jesus who died for us so that we can be winners over our sin.

Session 4

Talking to Your Father

SESSION GOALS:

D.I.V.A. participants will:
- Understand the importance of prayer as critical to strengthening their relationship with God
- Learn a basic template for prayer
- Participate in an activity to illustrate a biblical design for prayer

SCRIPTURE FOCUS:

Matthew 6:5-15 (NLT); Matthew 7:7-12, Matthew 18:20

MATERIALS NEEDED:

- D.I.V.A. Handbooks, one book for each girl
- Bibles: Inform the girls to bring Bibles if they have them
- Blank paper (four sheets, plus a few extras in case mistakes are made)
- Smooth rock for each girl (should be large enough to write a small word on it, but small enough to carry in pocket or purse; available at dollar store or craft store in home decoration section)
- Thin-tip permanent markers (enough for the girls to share during the session)

PREP TASKS:

NONE

RECALL (if applicable)

If applicable, follow the directions for facilitating the recall segment described in the introduction on page 18.

CHECK –IN

Make up your own Check-In activity or facilitate the "Highs and Lows" Check-In activity described in the introduction on page 17.

FOUNDATION

Share with the group:

Today we are talking about how to pray. Prayer is essential to developing our relationship with God. We cannot grow stronger in our faith if we don't pray. There are many ways to pray. Some prayers are short, some prayers are long. Sometimes we pray for ourselves, and at other times we pray for others. We don't have to speak a certain way to pray. We can talk to God, just as we speak to each other in this group. We want to be careful not to use God as a "genie in a bottle," just praying when we are in trouble and want something. He wants to hear from us when things are going good and bad. He really loves when his children come to Him in prayer.

Ask the group:

- How many people think you pray enough?
- Why do you think it is so difficult to pray consistently to God?

Responses may revolve around not knowing what to say or how to use the right words.

Share with the group:

God gives us examples and instructions for how to pray in the Bible. If you know how to talk and listen, you know how to pray! Prayer is two-way communication. We talk to God and God speaks back to us in many ways. He speaks through His Word and the Holy Spirit within you. He may speak to you through a beautiful sunrise or the confirmation spoken from other believers. The point is that He can speak to you in any way He wants, but you will know it is Him speaking to you because it will be confirmed in the Bible.

This "speaking" from God usually will come to you as a thought in your own head, not necessarily an actual voice you can hear … although He could do that if He wanted! If it is different than what the Bible says, then you will know that it was not God speaking to you. Even if you find it in the Bible, you may still have to pray to ask God if it is a word for YOU. You will have to do some searching in His Word to confirm that was God speaking to you, and not just some thoughts you came up with on your own or that come from another source that isn't God! The more you read your Bible, pray, learn about God, and seek Him, you will learn about His character traits and become stronger at identifying when God is talking to you.

Ask someone to read Matthew 7:7-12

Ask and it will be given to you; seek and you will find; knock and the door will be opened to you. For everyone who asks receives; the one who seeks finds; and to the one who knocks, the door will be opened. "Which of you, if your son asks for bread, will give him a stone? Or if he asks for a fish, will give him a snake? If you, then, though you are evil, know how to give good gifts to your children, how much more will your Father in heaven give good gifts to those who ask him! So in everything, do to others what you would have them do to you, for this sums up the Law and the Prophets.

Share with the group:

This scripture basically says if you are looking for God, you will find Him. It also explains that we can pray for whatever our hearts want. If it will be good for us in God's eyes, He will give it to us. He uses the example of a father who gives good things to his children. Now this does not mean that God will give us everything we ask for. He wants the best for us. He always gives us what we need, and often gives us the things we want.

Sometimes He says "no" to protect us from ourselves and some of the crazy stuff we've asked for. If God gives us everything we ask for, we would be messed up! We sometimes don't know what we need for right now, but God can see now and down the street and around the corner before we even get there!

Ask the group for examples of things they've asked for (whether if asked to a parent/ friend/other person or to God in prayer), and then realized later it was not good for them. Discuss their responses. Provide an example of your own if the group has difficulty coming up with examples.

Share with the group:

Fortunately, for those of us who have a hard time praying, God provides a prayer template—like a recipe—for prayer in His Word. It's called the Lord's Prayer.

Ask someone to read Matthew 6:5-15 (NLT)

"When you pray, don't be like the hypocrites who love to pray publicly on street corners and in the synagogues where everyone can see them. I tell you the truth, that is all the reward they will ever get. But when you pray, go away by yourself, shut the door behind you, and pray to your Father in private. Then your Father, who sees everything, will reward you. "When you pray, don't babble on and on as people of other religions do. They think their prayers are answered merely by repeating their words again and again. Don't be like them, for your Father knows exactly what you need even before you ask him! Pray like this:

Our Father in heaven, may your name be kept holy. May your Kingdom come soon. May your will be done on earth, as it is in heaven. Give us today the food we need, and forgive us our sins, as we have forgiven those who sin against us. And don't let us yield to temptation, but rescue us from the evil one. "If you forgive those who sin against you, your heavenly Father will forgive you. But if you refuse to forgive others, your Father will not forgive your sins.

Share with the group:

Jesus gives us instructions for how to pray and what to include in our prayers. For 'how to pray,' He tells us not to pray long show-off prayers to impress others, but to pray in private (in "secret") to God. This does not mean we can't pray with others, such as when we pray together in church, with our families, or in our D.I.V.A. group. Matthew 18:20 says, "For where two or three gather in my name, there am I with them." The main point is that prayer should be for real, not for showing off. Jesus offers the Lord's Prayer as instructions for what we should include in our prayers. We don't necessarily have to use these exact statements, but the type of statements in the prayer is what we can model our prayers after. We can break it down to four types of statements that are good to include in every prayer—statements that show love for God, ask for forgiveness, thank God for His love, and ask God for the things we need.

Review what to include in prayer using the excerpts below from the Lord's Prayer (girls can follow along in the D.I.V.A. Handbook):

LOVE- *To show God your personal love and respect for Him and that you acknowledge His greatness. God loves for us to tell Him that we love Him. That's why He created us. "Our Father in heaven.*

Imagine if your parents or someone else you love, never told you that they love you. Even if know someone loves you, you still like to hear them say it because it feels good. God is the same way. He knows what's in your heart, but He wants to hear it anyway.

Ask the group, "How can you tell God you love Him?" (Responses may include singing, dancing, or just saying 'I love you.')

Explain that there are lots of ways to tell God you love Him. This could include telling Him WHY you love Him. Ask the group for examples of why they love God. (Responses may include "because He woke me up," "He helped me out of a bad situation," etc. – Provide your own examples here.)

Explain that you also show your love by telling Him WHO He is to you. Examples include the names of God, i.e. Creator, Jehovah-Jireh (Provider), Jehovah-Ropha (Healer), etc.

Share with the group:

We can always say "I love you!" to God in our prayers. Sometimes we may do it by saying His names, or by singing a song, or by restating the things He's done for us. However we say it, He wants to hear it from us!

FORGIVENESS – To realize that our sin is against God's will, so we need to ask for

forgiveness and repent. Remember sin left unchecked can cause separation from God (See session 3). We have to confess so that our relationship with God isn't hurt. "Forgive us our debts, as we also forgive our debtors."

We also have to forgive others so that God can forgive us. "For if you forgive other people when they sin against you, your heavenly Father will also forgive you. But if you do not forgive others their sins, your Father will not forgive your sins."

Share with the group:

Think about if you got into a fight with your best friend, and you knew you were wrong. If you didn't tell your friend that you were sorry, over time that would start to hurt your friendship with him or her. It's the same way with God. Tell Him you are sorry every time you do something that you are not supposed to do. He loves to hear your confession, and He will fix your relationship with Him right away.

THANKS – To show appreciation and gratefulness for what He has done and who He is to you. "Hallowed be your name." Hallow means holy.

Share with the group:

You would get pretty frustrated if you did something nice for someone, and they didn't even say thank you, right? Well, we forget to tell God thank you all the time for the great things He does for us. If you can't think of anything to be thankful for, just thank Him for waking you up this morning and putting people that love you in your life.

48

NEED– To petition God on behalf of yourself and others for things you need Him to do. "Give us today our daily bread." "And lead us not into temptation, but deliver us from the evil one."

Share with the group:

This is the easy part! We never forget to ask God for what we need. In addition, to asking God for our needs, we should also ask for the needs of others.

ACTIVITY: *LFTN ("Lifting") Up Your Voice*

Share with the group:

So now that you know the parts of prayer, let's practice!

Divide the girls into four groups. Assign each group a letter of the prayer acronym (L – F – T – N). Give each group a sheet of paper and marker. Based on the information shared in the foundation section above, instruct the group to come up with a phrase (four words or less) they could use in prayer for the letter they have been assigned. For example, for "L," they may write "I love you" or "God you are awesome." For "F" they may write, "Lord I'm sorry." For "T," they may write "Thank you Lord." For "N," they may write "Please help me." Encourage the girls to be creative. If any group is struggling to come up with a phrase, assist them with coming up with one. Give everyone a maximum of 5-10 minutes to brainstorm and write down their phrase.

Have the entire group read each sign as you point to each group. Do that a few times, so everyone will say all the phrases. Now, tell them that sincere prayer is music to God's ears; they will be the orchestra, and you will be the conductor. When you point to them, each group will lift up their sign and say (or sing!) the phrase they have on the paper. Only the group that wrote the phrase will hold it up and say it when you point to each group. Tell them that the four phrases represent the four parts of prayer that are good to say to God every time we pray.

Act like a conductor and begin to random point to each group. Slow down and speed up for a fun effect on the "song."

Say to the group, "Sometimes my prayers may be a little different based on if I'm really going through something." Point to the groups in order (L-F-T-N) and then keep pointing to the "N" group so they can keep repeating their request.

Say to the group, "And sometimes I'm overwhelmed by everything He's done for me, so my prayers are like this…" Point to the groups and keep pointing to the "T" group so they can keep repeating their thanks.

Say to the group, "And does anyone ever have prayers like this when they know they really messed up?" Point to the groups and keep pointing to the "F" group, so they can keep repeating their apology to God.

Play with the sequence and repetition to reinforce the concept until you think the group has an understanding.

DISCUSSION

In their small groups, have the girls discuss which areas their prayers are lacking in (L-F-T-N). After they discuss, come back as a large group and have each group share.

D.I.V.A. CHALLENGE

Distribute the rocks and ask each girl to use a marker to write one word on her rock that represents an area she needs prayer in (i.e. grades; for prayer to do better in school). Instruct the girls to switch rocks with another girl.

Share with the group:

The D.I.V.A. Challenge for this week is to pray for one of your fellow D.I.V.A.s over the week. The rock represents a strong foundation on which we can build our lives. Prayer, God's word, and our faith are our strong foundation to build our lives upon. You should keep this rock with you for the entire week. Carry it in your purse or in your pocket. Whenever you see it, say a prayer for your partner and the area where they need prayer. It doesn't have to be a super long prayer, just a real sincere prayer. Pray like you are praying for yourself. Write about it in your handbook.

Tell the girls you will ask them to report on their progress with this challenge at the next session.

CLOSING REFLECTION & PRAYER

Share with the group:

Today we have shared some information that can help all of us strengthen our prayer life. To make prayer become a habit, it may be helpful to set a time and place every day to pray when you won't be distracted. For example, pray in your room first thing when you get up in the morning and when you go to bed. Read a few scriptures in your Bible when you do it to really step it up. Start with 5-10 minutes each day, and increase the time as you grow in your faith.

Invite a girl to pray out loud for the group using the L-F-T-N format. End the session with this prayer:

Father, we love you! Forgive us for not praying to you as often as we should. Thank you for being patient with us, and for giving us more knowledge of you to strengthen our faith. Build a thirst in us for you, so that spending time with you in prayer will become an everyday part of our lives. Help us, Lord, to read our Word more and to realize when you are speaking to us. Help us to pray for others, as well as ourselves. You are an awesome God!

Session 5

New Identity

SESSION GOALS:

D.I.V.A. participants will:

- Understand what it means to be "dead to self" and "alive in Christ"
- Learn to embrace their new identity as a disciple of Christ

SCRIPTURE FOCUS:

Genesis 1:27 (NLT); Romans 12:1-2 (NLT); Galatians 5:22-25 (NLT); Romans 6:11-14; Colossians 3:5-14

MATERIALS NEEDED:

- D.I.V.A. Handbooks, one book for each girl
- Bibles: Inform the girls to bring Bibles if they have them
- "If They Really Knew Me" Activity
- Colored pencils
- Cardboard box to represent a casket (can be shoe box size or larger for visual effect).
- Small note size paper or post-its

PREP TASKS:

- Copy the "If They Really Knew Me" worksheet for each girl.
- Write on the "casket" or make a sign to put on it that says, "Here Lies the Old Ways of the Destined D.I.V.A.s"

RECALL (if applicable)

If applicable, follow the directions for facilitating the recall segment described in the introduction on page 18.

CHECK –IN

Make up your own Check-In activity or facilitate the "Highs and Lows" Check-In activity described in the introduction on page 17.

GETTING STARTED

Share with the group:
Today we are going to talk about our identity and our image as children of God.

Ask the group, "What's the difference between our image and our identity?" Discuss their responses.

Share with the group:

Our image is the "picture" we show the world about who we are. Our identity is made up of the personality traits that set us apart from others—our uniqueness and individuality. Sometimes you may feel frustrated or misunderstood when the picture that people see (image) doesn't match up with who you really are (identity). Sometimes our image and identity don't match up because we act in ways that really don't represent who we are. Sometimes it is because people stereotype you and make their own picture up about who you are, regardless of what you show them.

ACTIVITY: If They Really Knew Me...

Pass out the worksheet. Using the colored pencils, instruct the girls to use words and/or pictures to complete each side of the worksheet. For example, someone may write "People think I have a bad attitude" on the left side, and "I'm really a very friendly person" on the right side. Encourage the girls to come up with as many examples as possible. Give them about 15 minutes to complete the exercise individually. Then,

allow the girls to share what they wrote on their paper with the group if they feel comfortable.

Ask the group, "Why do you think people see you in these ways, if this is not who you really are?" Discuss their responses.

 Listen for explanations that indicate that they are acting in ways that are not consistent with their identity as children of God. Then ask the group, "Do you think this is connected in any way to your identity as a child of God?" Discuss their responses.

FOUNDATION

Share with the group:

As children of God, our image and identity should look very similar; however, the things we show the world do not always match up to the characteristics that Christ wants us to display.

Ask for volunteers to read the following scriptures, and share the comments provided between each scripture.

Genesis 1:27 (NLT)
So God created human beings in his own image.In the image of God he created them; male and female he created them.

Share with the group:

God created us to look like Him! When we accept Christ as our Lord and Savior, we are making a choice to show the world characteristics in us that represent God. This is what is meant by letting your light shine.

Ask someone to read Galatians 5:22-25(NLT)

But the fruit of the Spirit is love, joy, peace, forbearance, kindness, goodness, faithfulness, gentleness and self-control. Against such things there is no law. Those who belong to Christ Jesus have crucified the flesh with its passions and desires. Since we live by the Spirit, let us keep in step with the Spirit.

Share with the group:

When we accept Christ, we receive the Holy Spirit, who lives inside of us (See session 2 on salvation). Characteristics such as love, joy, peace, and self-control are evidence that God's spirit is inside of us. This is part of the image we should be showing the world. These are also characteristics that show others that we have an identity as a child of God. Just as you may have eyes or a similar laugh like your biological father, you should also have some traits that are similar to your Heavenly Father.

Ask someone to read Romans 12:1-2 (NLT)

And so, dear brothers and sisters, I plead with you to give your bodies to God because of all he has done for you. Let them be a living and holy sacrifice—the kind he will find acceptable. This is truly the way to worship him. Don't copy the behavior and customs of this world, but let God transform you into a new person by changing the way you think. Then you will learn to know God's will for you, which is good and pleasing and perfect.

Share with the group:

We do not belong to ourselves. God does not require us to sacrifice things to him, as people had to do in the Old Testament before Jesus died for our sins. Now, WE are the sacrifice, as we live our lives and try to show an image that looks like God. Every day of our lives, we should be striving to make everything we do—the way we speak, the way we act, and even what we think about—be an opportunity to thank God for His love for us. This is our daily sacrifice to God. And slowly as we learn more about God and His ways, we will change to become more like Him and we will start to think about our lives and the world differently. This is what "renewing of your mind" means—a new perspective.

Ask someone to read Romans 6:11-14 (NLT)

So you also should consider yourselves to be dead to the power of sin and alive to God through Christ Jesus. Do not let sin control the way you live; do not give in to sinful desires. Do not let any part of your body become an instrument of evil to serve sin. Instead, give yourselves completely to God, for you were dead, but now you have new life. So use your whole body as an instrument to do what is right for the glory of God. Sin is no longer your master, for you no longer live under the requirements of the law. Instead, you live under the freedom of God's grace.

Ask the group, "So, if we don't belong to ourselves, who do we belong to?" They will mostly likely respond with "God."

Share with the group:

Yes! We belong to God. This is what the scriptures mean by "Dead to Self, Alive in Christ." Our own selfish desires, which often lead us away from God, shouldn't be calling the shots in our lives! God's way of doing things is our new way of living. It makes Him angry when unbelievers reject Him, and when believers continue to do things the old way. God tells us to kill those old ways of doing things. The only things that matter are the things we do for Christ. If we are serious about living for Christ, we must show it! When we know better, we must do better!

Ask someone to read Colossians 3:5-14

Put to death, therefore, whatever belongs to your earthly nature: sexual immorality, impurity, lust, evil desires and greed, which is idolatry. Because of these, the wrath of God is coming. You used to walk in these ways, in the life you once lived. But now you must also rid yourselves of all such things as these: anger, rage, malice, slander, and filthy language from your lips. Do not lie to each other, since you have taken off your old self with its practices and have put on the new self, which is being renewed in knowledge in the image of its Creator. Here there is no Gentile or Jew, circumcised or uncircumcised, barbarian, Scythian, slave or free, but Christ is all, and is in all. Therefore, as God's chosen people, holy and dearly loved, clothe yourselves with compassion, kindness, humility, gentleness and patience. Bear

with each other and forgive one another if any of you has a grievance against someone. Forgive as the Lord forgave you. And over all these virtues put on love, which binds them all together in perfect unity.

ACTIVITY: Bury It!

Set up the "casket" and tell the girls, "We are about to have a funeral for the 'old ways' that we need to put to death." Hand out the small pieces of paper, and ask the girls to write their 'old ways' on the paper. Give them a few minutes to write them down. Instruct the girls to line up to "bury" their 'old ways' in the casket.

DISCUSSION

Based on the activity, lead the girls in a discussion using the following prompts:
- What will you gain from burying some of these old ways? In your earthly life? In your spiritual life? (For example, by burying an 'old way' of lying to one's parents about their whereabouts after school, they may gain their parents trust and a stronger relationship with them).
- What help will you need to turn away from these old ways?
- Who can you ask for help to keep you accountable?

D.I.V.A. CHALLENGE

Share with the group:

The D.I.V.A. Challenge for this week is to 1.) Read Colossians 3:1-17; and 2.) Work on your image this week and make a special effort to put one of your 'old ways' to death. Write about it in your handbook.

Tell the girls you will ask them to report on their progress with this challenge at the next session.

CLOSING REFLECTION & PRAYER

Share with the group:

The casket activity represents what God wants us to do with our old ways that do not make Him happy. The real work is actually starting to kill these ways in our real lives. It probably won't happen overnight, but each day make an effort to move closer to living for Christ in every area of your life.

Invite a girl to pray out loud for the group based on the topic discussed. End the session with this prayer:

Father, you are such a merciful God! Thank you for the freedom you give us to bury our old ways and be made new in Jesus Christ. Change our perspective as we spend more time with you in prayer and reading the Word. Help us to see the world and our lives through your eyes. Make this Word come alive in us. Hide it in our hearts so that we will try every day to bury our old ways. Thank you for your grace towards us.

Session 5 Activity: If They _Really_ Knew Me...

If people really knew me, they would see this when look at me:

This is what people see when they look at me:

STAND OUT
Sessions 6-8

Theme Overview:

This theme centers on how to stand out for Christ versus just falling in line with the crowd. A central key scripture for all the sessions in this theme is 1 Peter 2:9:

"But you are a chosen people, a royal priesthood, a holy nation, God's special possession, that you may declare the praises of him who called you out of darkness into his wonderful light."

Through these sessions, girls are encouraged to take off the "masks" they wear to impress others; be authentic by living out their integrity; examine their value systems based on God's Word; discuss some of the challenges of being committed to Christ; and discuss issues like peer pressure and gossip which may challenge their attempts to stand out for Christ. Above all, through continuing to learn about God in the context of group fellowship and support, the girls will learn that they are special and chosen by God to stand out of the crowd for Christ!

Session 6

Take off the Mask

SESSION GOALS:

D.I.V.A. participants will:

- Understand that God calls them to be separate from the crowd
- Explore areas where they "wear a mask" to look like everyone else
- Be encouraged to be authentic for Christ

SCRIPTURE FOCUS:

1 Peter 2:9; Romans 12:1-2 (NLT)

MATERIALS NEEDED:

- D.I.V.A. Handbooks, one book for each girl
- Bibles: Inform the girls to bring Bibles if they have them
- Take Off the Mask Worksheet
- Colored pencils or markers
- Scissors (enough for the girls to share)
- Hole puncher (enough for the girls to share)
- String or yarn (enough for everyone's mask)

PREP TASKS:

- Copy the Take Off the Mask Worksheet for each girl

RECALL (if applicable)

If applicable, follow the directions for facilitating the recall segment described in the introduction on page 18.

CHECK –IN

Make up your own Check-In activity or facilitate the "Highs and Lows" Check-In activity described in the introduction on page 17.

FOUNDATION

Share with the group:

Today we will be discussing God's desire for us to stand out for Him. We will discuss our image, values, and integrity; and how we sometimes wear a "mask" that hides who we really are. (Refer back to the image and identity concepts in session 5 if the group has already covered that session.)

Ask someone to read 1 Peter 2:9:

But you are a chosen people, a royal priesthood, a holy nation, God's special possession, that you may declare the praises of him who called you out of darkness into his wonderful light.

Share with the group:

In the King James Version of this scripture, it uses the phrase "peculiar people," instead of "God's special possession."

Ask the group, "Does anyone know what peculiar means?" Allow the girls to respond.

Share with the group:

Peculiar means different from the usual or normal; special; distinctive; odd. Usually "odd" refers to something that is "separate" or "without a match," such as an "odd sock" or the "odd man out" when someone doesn't have a partner. Now, does this mean that God wants us to be weird loners? No, this means that we are not created to just go along with what everyone else is doing, especially if it doesn't allow us to shine our light and show God within us. Sometimes we may have to go alone. Sometimes we will not be able to partner up with the people around us if their path is not leading to Christ.

Ask someone to read Romans 12:1-2 (NLT)

And so, dear brothers and sisters, I plead with you to give your bodies to God because of all he has done for you. Let them be a living and holy sacrifice—the

kind he will find acceptable. This is truly the way to worship him. Don't copy the behavior and customs of this world, but let God transform you into a new person by changing the way you think. Then you will learn to know God's will for you, which is good and pleasing and perfect.

Share with the group:

We were created to follow God's Word and not the crowd that may not know Him. We were created to be a light to others that are still trying to find Him. Sometimes, especially when you are young (and even when your old!), it's hard to be different...to not be a part of the crowd. God will give us strength. We are being changed as we are gaining a new perspective based on God's Word and love for us. This is what it means by "the renewing of your mind."

Sometimes because it is uncomfortable to be "peculiar," we wear a "mask" to hide who we really are. This could be hiding our faith in God, hiding our true feelings because we want to fit in, or hiding by not speaking the truth about what is going on in our lives. We are going to do an exercise to discuss the masks that we wear.

ACTIVITY: Take Off the Mask

Pass out the activity sheets and colored pencils/markers. Instruct the girls to use words and/or pictures to draw on the mask to represent how they are "looking like the crowd" or wearing a mask to blend in with everyone else. Give them about 15 minutes to draw on the masks. Then distribute the scissors, and tell them to cut out their masks. Circulate the hole punchers. Instruct them to punch a hole on both sides of the mask, and attach enough string so that they can tie their masks on them. Go around the group and give each girl a turn to present the words/pictures on her mask. After each girl presents, tell her to tie her mask on. After everyone has shared and put on their masks, ask the girls to describe what it feels like to wear their mask. Some girls make take it literal and give responses like silly, fun, or stupid. Other girls may connect on a more symbolic level based on the words/pictures on their masks. They may use powerful words to describe their experiences, such as lonely, sad, angry, hypocritical, imprisoned, etc.

Share with the group:

It doesn't feel good to wear a mask all the time. It can feel like you are tied up and are not free to be yourself. Through our Lord and Savior Jesus Christ, we have freedom to be who He created us to be. We don't have to hide the beauty of our words, thoughts, or actions when we are living to represent Christ. We don't have to wear a mask anymore.

Instruct the girls to take off their masks and tear them up.

Share with the group:

Tearing up the mask is a symbol that we understand that we don't have to be locked up by trying to look like everyone else. This will not be easy, but this activity represents our understanding of the masks we've been wearing. We will now make every effort to let our true selves shine through to the world. This is what is meant by the phrase, "in the world, but not of the world." We know that we live and move in the world each day, but we also know that our goal is to make our lives look like God's will is for us, and not what everyone else says we should do.

DISCUSSION

Based on the activity, lead the girls in a discussion using the following prompts:

- In what areas is it the most difficult for you to stand out from the crowd?
- What role does peer pressure play in wearing our masks?
- Are there any consequences or prices you've had to pay for going along with the crowd?
- What would it really take for you to tear up your mask and step out of the crowd in these areas? What type of support would you need?
- In what areas do you find it easier to be the leader and influencer of others?
- What can you do to be even more of a positive influence in these areas?

D.I.V.A. CHALLENGE

Share with the group:

The D.I.V.A. Challenge for this week is to 1.) Read and reflect on 1 Peter 2:9 several times throughout the week; and 2.) Make a focused effort on standing out from the crowd in one of your difficult areas this week. Write about it in your handbook. Pray about it throughout the week.

Tell the girls you will ask them to report on their progress with this challenge at the next session.

CLOSING REFLECTION & PRAYER

Share with the group:

Remember, tearing up your masks today represent the freedom we have in Jesus Christ to be who He has created us to be. Stand out!

Invite a girl to pray out loud for the group based on the topic discussed. End the session with this prayer:

Father, thank you for the freedom you offered us when Jesus Christ died on the cross for our sin. Forgive us for times when we have not listened to your Holy Spirit inside of us telling us to stand out from the crowd. Help us to listen to you and to have courage to walk in the purpose that you have for our lives. We love you, Lord. Help us to do better. Help us to take off our masks.

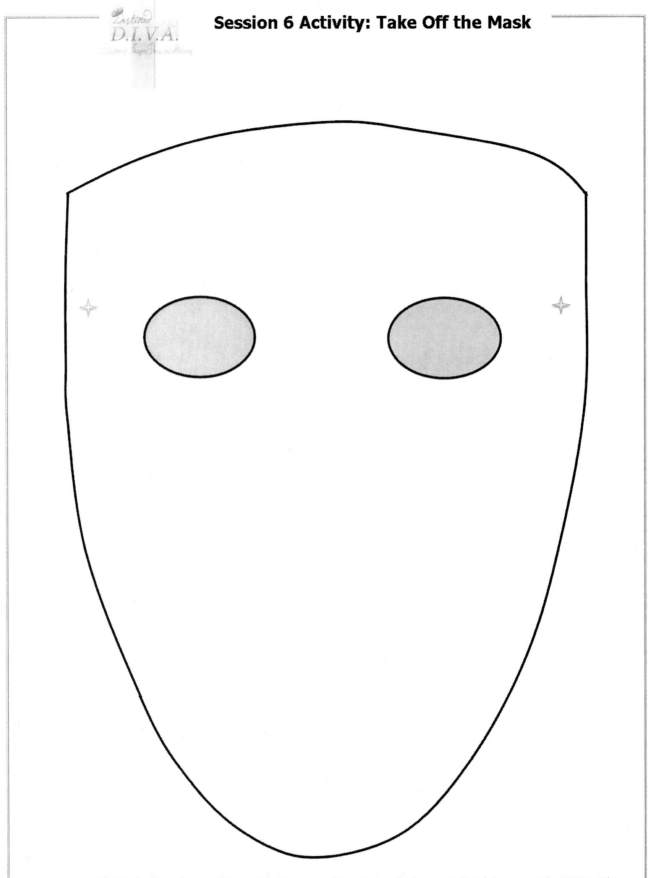

Session 7

Walking with Christ

SESSION GOALS:

D.I.V.A. participants will:

• Understand that it requires commitment to grow in one's faith and personal relationship with God

• Explore their personal commitment to living according to God's Word

• Discuss the challenges and joys of being a disciple of Christ

SCRIPTURE FOCUS:

Ephesians 6:14-15 (NLT); 1 Peter 2:9; James 1:22-25; 1 John 2:5-6

See also Ephesians 6:10-20

MATERIALS NEEDED:

· D.I.V.A. Handbooks, one book for each girl

· Bibles: Inform the girls to bring Bibles if they have them

· Long piece of banner paper or several pieces of paper taped together, decorated as a road (black with yellow dotted stripe down the middle)

· Walking with Christ Handout

· Tape

PREP TASKS:

· Make several copies of the Walking with Christ Activity, and cut out the shoe pictures so that you have more than one copy of each type of shoe.

· Hang up the "road" on the wall for the "Which Shoes are You Wearing?" activity

----

RECALL (if applicable)

If applicable, follow the directions for facilitating the recall segment described in the introduction on page 18.

CHECK –IN

Make up your own Check-In activity or facilitate the "Highs and Lows" Check-In activity described in the introduction on page 17.

63

FOUNDATION

Share with the group:

Today we will discuss being committed to God. Through our journey to learn more about Christ and become more like Him, we will go through many joys and challenges on our Christian walk. However, being a disciple of Christ requires us to keep trying to live according to God's Word, even when we fail.

Ask the group, "What's something you are committed to?" Discuss their responses, and then ask "How do you know that you are committed to something? What would someone else observe from watching you, to come to the conclusion that you are committed to that particular thing? Discuss their responses.

Share with the group:

Common characteristics to show your commitment to something include: your willingness to sacrifice things for it, willingness to stick with it, and it is something that's valued in your life. Eventually there are rewards that come from it. Think of professional athletes who work long hours preparing to play. The athletes are sacrificing time that could be spent with their families. Even if they lose a game, they stick with it and practice harder so they can win the next one. They value the sport as their career, and know that with hard works they eventually will win the game. These same characteristics apply to our walk with Christ.

Ask someone to read Ephesians 6:14-15(NLT)

Stand your ground, putting on the belt of truth and the body armor of God's righteousness. For shoes, put on the peace that comes from the Good News so that you will be fully prepared.

Share with the group:

We can only be ready to walk this challenging road as Christians by reading our Bible to get instructions on what God wants us to do. This is what is meant by "readiness that comes from the gospel of peace." The gospel of peace is God's Word.

Ask someone to read 1 Peter 2:9:

But you are a chosen people, a royal priesthood, a holy nation, God's special possession, that you may declare the praises of him who called you out of darkness into his wonderful light.

Share with the group:

When walking with Christ, we will sometimes have to stand out from the crowd to follow God's Word. God chose us to show His light to others. He has strong words for those that confess that they are His children, but do not do his Word.

Ask someone to read James 1:22-25

Do not merely listen to the word, and so deceive yourselves. Do what it says. Anyone who listens to the word but does not do what it says is like someone who looks at his face in a mirror and, after looking at himself, goes away and immediately forgets what he looks like. But whoever looks intently into the perfect law that gives freedom, and continues in it

—not forgetting what they have heard, but doing it—they will be blessed in what they do.

1 John 2:4-6 (The Message)
If someone claims, "I know him well!" but doesn't keep his commandments, he's obviously a liar. His life doesn't match his words. But the one who keeps God's word is the person in whom we see God's mature love. This is the only way to be sure we're in God. Anyone who claims to be intimate with God ought to live the same kind of life Jesus lived.

Share with the group:

From this, it is clear that we cannot know who we are as God's children without reading and DOING God's Word. This is what is meant by the reference to walking away from the mirror and forgetting what we look like. The Bible is our mirror because it shows us the characteristics of God. We are His children. He wants us to look like Him in the way we act in the world. It also gives us a really tough message that if we don't do what God's Word says, we don't know God. Ouch! That hurt, but our walk with Christ is serious business. I want to know God! If you do too, we must try each day to do what His Word says.

ACTIVITY: Which Shoes Are You Wearing?

Share with group:

We are going to do an activity to help us reflect on what our current walk with Christ looks like, and what we may need to do to strengthen our relationship with our Heavenly Father.

Hold up one of the pictures of each pair of shoes and explain the type of walk with Christ they represent using the following descriptions:

- **Flip Flops**—I accepted Christ, but I have been pretty lazy in my walk with Christ. I haven't put forth much effort.

- **Gym Shoes**—I was making an effort to "run" with Christ, but I got off track. I want to get it together and get back in the race.

- **Worn Out Shoes**—I feel like life is beating me down. I have been too overwhelmed to try and walk with Christ. I need help!

- **Work boots**—It has been really hard work, but I've been making solid efforts to let my light shine for Christ in my attitude, behavior, and communication with others.

- **High Heels**—I have "special event" faith. It's sparkly and shiny for the world to see on the outside, but on the inside I'm not really walking with Christ.

- **Barefoot**—I don't have shoes. I don't know if I am "saved." I haven't made a commitment to Christ.

Spread the multiple copies of pictures of shoes from the handout on the table. Have each girl select the shoe that currently represents her walk with Christ and tape it on the "road" on the wall. Encourage them to be honest, and remind the group that no one is there to judge anyone else.

Note: If the group meets regularly, keep the road and some of the shoe pictures. Periodically, ask the girls to reflect on their walk and if their "shoes" have changed. This is a good reflection exercise to help the girls see growth in their faith as they learn more about God and His Word.

DISCUSSION

Based on the activity, lead the girls in a discussion using the following prompts:
- What does it mean to walk with Christ?
- Share about the shoe you selected to represent your walk with Christ. Why did you select that picture?
- Do you like the "shoes" you are currently in? Which ones would you prefer to wear? What are you willing to sacrifice to wear those shoes?
- Based on our discussion earlier, would you say you have been committed to Christ?
- For those who are "barefoot," are you ready to accept Christ? (If so, see the S.A.Y. Outline at the end of this session)

D.I.V.A. CHALLENGE

Share with the group:

The D.I.V.A. Challenge for this week is to 1.) Read and reflect on 1 John 2:6, and Ephesians 6:10-20; and 2.) Think about a sacrifice you will need to make to walk with Christ. Try to put it in action. Write about it in your handbook. Pray about it throughout the week.

Tell the girls you will ask them to report on their progress with this challenge at the next session.

CLOSING REFLECTION & PRAYER

Share with the group:

The Word of God is our mirror. God clearly states in His Word that if we are just reading it and not DOING it, we do not know Him. To be truly committed to God, we have to try to live according to His Word.

Invite a girl to pray out loud for the group based on the topic discussed. End the session with this prayer:

Father, thank you for the opportunity you have given us to walk with you. Forgive us if we have not been committed to you. Help us to see sacrifice for your sake, as a wonderful opportunity to walk with you. We know there will be rewards here on Earth and in heaven. Help us to do better. Help us to read your Word more so we will learn how to become more like you.

If there are "barefoot" girls that would like to accept Jesus Christ as their Lord and Savior, review the key points of salvation using the S.A.Y. Outline (See Session 21 on page 159 for more details). Encourage the girls to say their own prayer of salvation. Help them if they are having difficulty, but allow them to come up with their own words.

Flip Flops—I accepted Christ, but I have been pretty lazy in my walk with Christ. I haven't put forth much effort.

Work Boots—It has been really hard work, but I've been making solid efforts to let my light shine for Christ in my attitude, behavior, and communication with others.

Gym Shoes—I made an effort to "run" with Christ, but I got off track here and there. I'm still trying to run the race.

High Heels—I have "special event" faith. It's sparkly and shiny for the world to see on the outside, but on the inside I'm not really walking with Christ.

Worn Out Shoes—I feel like life is beating me down. I have been too overwhelmed to try and walk with Christ. I need help!

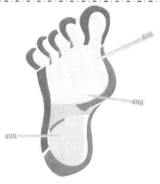

Barefoot—I don't even have shoes. I don't even know if I am "saved." I haven't made a commitment to Christ.

Session 8

Decisions, Decisions

SESSION GOALS:

D.I.V.A. participants will:
- Explore different decision-making styles
- Learn a basic problem-solving strategy
- Understand parameters given in God's Word for making decisions
- Practice applying God's Word to real life situations

SCRIPTURE FOCUS:

- Romans 7:17-23, 25 (MSG);

See also 1 Corinthians 13; Philippians 3:14; Matthew 5:14-16

MATERIALS NEEDED:

- D.I.V.A. Handbooks, one book for each girl
- Bibles: Inform the girls to bring Bibles if they have them
- Flip chart paper
- Markers
- Decisions, Decisions Scenarios Handout
- Decision-Making Worksheet
- Decisions, Decisions reminder cards

PREP TASKS:

- Write the decision-making styles on the flip chart paper and post in the room
- Cut the scenarios out for the group skit activity
- Copy the decision-making worksheets – one for each girl
- Write the steps to responsible decision-making discussed in the session on a piece of flip chart paper. Do not post the paper until instructed later in the session
- Print the Decisions, Decisions reminder cards (2 pages , print double-sided) on card stock and cut them out to provide a copy to each girl

----

RECALL (if applicable)

If applicable, follow the directions for facilitating the recall segment described in the introduction on page 18.

CHECK –IN

Make up your own Check-In activity or facilitate the "Highs and Lows" Check-In activity described in the introduction on page 17.

FOUNDATION

Share with the group:

Today we will discuss solving problems and making decisions. As Christians, we have an instruction manual for life in the Bible. However, our Heavenly Father always gives us a choice, an opportunity to do the right thing.

Ask someone to read Romans 7:17-23, 25
THE MESSAGE:

But I need something more! For if I know the law but still can't keep it, and if the power of sin within me keeps sabotaging my best intentions, I obviously need help! I realize that I don't have what it takes. I can will it, but I can't do it. I decide to do good, but I don't really do it; I decide not to do bad, but then I do it anyway. My decisions, such as they are, don't result in actions. Something has gone wrong deep within me and gets the better of me every time. It happens so regularly that it's predictable. The moment I decide to do good, sin is there to trip me up. I truly delight in God's commands, but it's pretty obvious that not all of me joins in that delight. Parts of me covertly rebel, and just when I least expect it, they take charge. The answer, thank God, is that Jesus Christ can and does. He acted to set things right in this life of contradictions where I want to serve God with all my heart and mind, but am pulled by the
influence of sin to do something totally different.

Share with the group:

Sometimes the answers are not so clear, and it is very difficult to figure out the right thing to do. Sin and what we desire have such a pull on us. Even when we want to do the right thing, we could end up making a horribly wrong decision because our human desire is often to do what WE want and not what GOD wants. This often leads us right to sin. Thank God for Jesus! When He died for us on the cross and rose again, He gave us power to practice self-control and to do what God wants us to do.

Ask the group if anyone can relate to wanting to do the right thing, but still doing the wrong thing. Ask them to share their experiences. Discuss their responses.

Share with the group:

Because God gives us the opportunity to make our own choices, we must take personal responsibility for the choices we make. Personal responsibility means we have to answer for the choices we make. This includes taking ownership of the mistakes, consequences, and rewards that may result from our choices. The best choice is a conscious and informed decision. This means that you are aware that a choice exists and you have the right information to help you make the best choice.

Review the decision-making styles you have posted in the room. As you discuss each style, ask the group for real-life examples in which they have used a particular style of decision-making.

- **Stalled decision-making** – Fear, procrastination, laziness, or disinterest takes over and you fail to make the decision or wait too long to make a decision often causing a negative effect.

- **Puppet decision-making** – You allow other people to make decisions for you. Imagine a puppet master pulling the strings to control the puppet. The puppet has no control over the actions taken. This could result in a negative or positive effect.

  Sometimes you may have no choice in this matter, like when your parents make choices for you with your best interest in mind. For example, your dad's job may be relocating and you have to move with your family. Other times, you may have a choice, but you allow someone else to influence it or make it for you. For example, all your friends are cheating on a test, and you don't say anything when someone looks over at your test to copy off your answers.

- **Responsible decision-making** – You think about the decision to be made before acting. You come with a number of actions you might take and consider the benefits of each. You pray about the decision and ask trusted adults for feedback, and you take responsibility for the consequences of the action.

Share with the group:

Outside of decisions that must be made by your parents or other trusted adults in your life, responsible decision-making is the best style!

Post the pre-written sheet you have prepared with the steps to responsible decision-making (Note: You do not have to write all the comments provided for each step below, just the main idea. However, you should provide some of the comments when verbally discussing the steps with the group.) Use one of the real-life examples shared by the girls to review each step of the decision-making process. As a group, walk through the selected example using the steps below.

7 Steps for responsible decision-making:

1. Name the problem – What is the real problem here? Call it exactly what it is.

   Sometimes the real problem may be "under the surface" and not what people are really dealing with. For example, the cause of a girl's poor attitude could be because her parents are going through a divorce and it is stressful for her, not because she just wants to be disrespectful and/or rude. Other times, the real problem may be exactly what is seen on a surface level.

2. Pray and search your Bible to help solve this problem – Ask God to help you see the issue as He sees it. Ask Him to give you wisdom to make the right decision. Ask Him for forgiveness if you have done something wrong to cause the problem. Thank Him for

giving you what you need to handle the problem correctly.

3. Think of all possible solutions that may be used to solve this problem. Don't judge the solutions at this step in the process; just brainstorm a list of all possible options to handle the issue.

4. List the positives and negatives of each possible solution to think about what consequences and rewards you may face when choosing a solution.

5. Find a trusted wise adult from your family, church, or school that you can discuss the issue with to get their opinion.

6. Pick a solution and do it.

7. Evaluate if that particular solution was the right choice based on the outcome. Think about the lessons you have learned about yourself and your decisions as a result of this process. Pray and thank God for letting you learn this lesson.

ACTIVITY: Ready, Think, Action!

Divide the girls into small groups, and distribute scenarios (one per group), worksheets (one per girl), and reminder cards (one per girl) to each group. Instruct the groups to discuss their scenarios and to apply the steps for responsible decision-making using the worksheet provided. Additionally, ask each group to select a scripture off the back of the reminder card (or another one they find themselves) that served as

inspiration for their solution. Lastly, each group will create a brief skit to show how they would address the issue in the scenario, and present it back to the large group. Tell them they have 15 minutes to discuss the scenario and prepare their skit before they present to the large group.

DISCUSSION

Based on the activity, lead the girls in a discussion using the following prompts:
- Ask each of the groups to provide a few points about why they selected the solutions demonstrated in their skits.
- Discuss their responses on the worksheets they completed as a group, and the scriptures that applied to their scenario.
- What are some factors that influence our decision making?
- How comfortable do you feel going to a trusted adult to discuss some of these issues?

Review the bullet points for good decision-making from a Christian perspective. Instruct the girls to look at these points on their reminder cards. If possible, recall specific examples from the skits that illustrate these points. As you read them, ask the girls if it is difficult to practice these points in real life. Why or why not?

- You rely on God's wisdom, not just your own (James 1:5)
- You ask for forgiveness when you are wrong (1 John 1:9)
- You try to look like Jesus—He is our example! What would Jesus Do?
- You try to let your light shine for Christ

(Matthew 5:14-16)
- You show love to others (Luke 6: 27-28, 31)
- You act based on your faith, not fear (2 Tim. 1:7, Hebrews 11:6)

D.I.V.A. CHALLENGE

Share with the group:

The D.I.V.A. Challenge for this week is to 1.) Read and reflect on the scriptures on the back of the reminder card; and 2.) Carry your reminder card this week, and attempt to use the responsible decision-making steps on a real problem you face this week. Write about it in your handbook. Pray about it throughout the week.

Tell the girls you will ask them to report on their progress with this challenge at the next session.

CLOSING REFLECTION & PRAYER

Share with the group:

Remember, although we are tempted at times to do the wrong thing, God gives us a choice. We have freedom in Christ to do the right thing, but we just have to make a decision to do it! Sometimes we will pass the test, and sometimes we will fail. God wants us to keep trying to do it His way.

Invite a girl to pray out loud for the group based on the topic discussed. End the session with this prayer:

Lord Jesus, thank you for the opportunity to come to you when we have a tough decision.

You are so faithful because even when we mess up, you forgive us, and wash us clean with your blood. Help us to learn your Word and hide it in our hearts, so we can begin to think like you when making decisions. Place adults and other young people in our lives that love you, so that we can have positive influences in the decisions we make. Keep us safe from danger. Build your wisdom in us each day. We will be so careful to thank you for all that you are doing for us.

Scenario 1—Your friend invites you to go to the mall. You don't have any money, and you know this person has shoplifted in the past. How would you handle this?

Scenario 2—You feel that your friend is trying to talk you into doing something you really do not want to do. You have a bad feeling about it. What would you do?

Scenario 3—A friend from school asks you over to study for mid-terms. You notice suspicious burns and bruises on her arm. She notices you've seen them and gets very nervous. What would you do?

Scenario 4—Your boyfriend broke up with you, and he is now dating your best friend. You are really angry about this. How would you handle this?

Scenario 5—You meet a guy you really like, but there is something about him that you do not quite trust. He invites you over to his house to hang out and watch a movie. Would you go?

Scenario 6—You find out your sister was talking about you behind your back. You are very angry and want to get her back for doing this. How will handle this?

Scenario 7—Your parents just pushed your curfew back to midnight. It is now 11:45 p.m.; you are out with your friends and do not want to go home. What will you do?

Scenario 8— You suspect your dad has a drinking problem. It makes you sad when he drinks. How will handle this?

Scenario 9— Your mom is getting married in two months to a man you just do not like. He tries hard to get to know you, but you never feel like talking to him. Your bad attitude is negatively affecting their relationship. What will you do?

Scenario 10— You are walking and find a wallet. Inside is $250 and identification. What will you do?

Session 8 Worksheet: Steps for Responsible Decision-Making

1. **Name the problem — What is the real problem here? Call it exactly what it is.**

2. **What specific things will you pray for when trying to find a solution to this problem?**

   Which Bible verse(s) gives you inspiration to solve this problem?

3. **List all solutions that may be used the solve this problem. Use back if necessary.**

4. **List the positives and negatives of each possible solution you listed.**

Solutions	Positives	Negatives
1.	1.	1.
	2.	2.
	3.	3.
2.	1.	1.
	2.	2.
	3.	3.
3.	1.	1.
	2.	2.
	3.	3.

5. **Who are wise, trusted adults from your family, church, or school you can ask about this?**

6. **Which solution will you put in action?**

7. **What lessons do you think you may learn from this experience?**

Destined D.I.V.A.
7 Steps for Responsible Decision-Making

1. Name the problem—Call it exactly what it is.
2. Pray and read your Bible to get answers.
3. Think of all possible solutions.
4. List the positives and negatives of each solution.
5. Find a trusted, wise adult to speak to about it.
6. Pick a solution and do it.
7. Evaluate if you picked the right solution. Ask yourself, "What lessons have I learned from this?"

Good Decision-Making Means…

- You rely on God's wisdom, not just your own (James 1:5)
- You ask for forgiveness when you are wrong (1 John 1:9)
- You try to look like Jesus—He is our example! What would Jesus Do?
- You try to let your light shine for Christ (Romans 12: 1-2)
- You show love to others (Luke 6: 27-28, 31)
- You act based on your faith, not fear (2 Tim. 1:7, Hebrews 11:6)

Destined D.I.V.A.
7 Steps for Responsible Decision-Making

1. Name the problem—Call it exactly what it is.
2. Pray and read your Bible to get answers.
3. Think of all possible solutions.
4. List the positives and negatives of each solution.
5. Find a trusted, wise adult to speak to about it.
6. Pick a solution and do it.
7. Evaluate if you picked the right solution. Ask yourself, "What lessons have I learned from this?"

Good Decision-Making Means…

- You rely on God's wisdom, not just your own (James 1:5)
- You ask for forgiveness when you are wrong (1 John 1:9)
- You try to look like Jesus—He is our example! What would Jesus Do?
- You try to let your light shine for Christ (Romans 12: 1-2)
- You show love to others (Luke 6: 27-28, 31)
- You act based on your faith, not fear (2 Tim. 1:7, Hebrews 11:6)

Destined D.I.V.A.
7 Steps for Responsible Decision-Making

1. Name the problem—Call it exactly what it is.
2. Pray and read your Bible to get answers.
3. Think of all possible solutions.
4. List the positives and negatives of each solution.
5. Find a trusted, wise adult to speak to about it.
6. Pick a solution and do it.
7. Evaluate if you picked the right solution. Ask yourself, "What lessons have I learned from this?"

Good Decision-Making Means…

- You rely on God's wisdom, not just your own (James 1:5)
- You ask for forgiveness when you are wrong (1 John 1:9)
- You try to look like Jesus—He is our example! What would Jesus Do?
- You try to let your light shine for Christ (Romans 12: 1-2)
- You show love to others (Luke 6: 27-28, 31)
- You act based on your faith, not fear (2 Tim. 1:7, Hebrews 11:6)

Scriptures to Think About

I can do all things through Christ who strengthens me. Philippians 4:13

For God hath not given us the spirit of fear, but of power, and of love, and of a sound mind. 2 Tim. 1:7

If we confess our sins, he is faithful and just and will forgive us our sins and purify us from all unrighteousness. 1 John 1:9

But to you who are listening I say: Love your enemies, do good to those who hate you, bless those who curse you, pray for those who mistreat you. Do to others as you would have them do to you. Luke 6: 27-28,31

...Everyone should be quick to listen, slow to speak and slow to become angry, because human anger does not produce the righteousness that God desires. James 1: 19-20

If any of you lacks wisdom, you should ask God, who gives generously to all without finding fault, and it will be given to you. James 1: 5

The tongue has the power of life and death, and those who love it will eat its fruit. Prov. 18:21

...offer your bodies as a living sacrifice, holy and pleasing to God—this is your true and proper worship. 2 Do not conform to the pattern of this world, but be transformed by the renewing of your mind. Then you will be able to test and approve what God's will is—his good, pleasing and perfect will. Romans 12: 1-2

Scriptures to Think About

I can do all things through Christ who strengthens me. Philippians 4:13

For God hath not given us the spirit of fear, but of power, and of love, and of a sound mind. 2 Tim. 1:7

If we confess our sins, he is faithful and just and will forgive us our sins and purify us from all unrighteousness. 1 John 1:9

But to you who are listening I say: Love your enemies, do good to those who hate you, bless those who curse you, pray for those who mistreat you. Do to others as you would have them do to you. Luke 6: 27-28,31

...Everyone should be quick to listen, slow to speak and slow to become angry, because human anger does not produce the righteousness that God desires. James 1: 19-20

If any of you lacks wisdom, you should ask God, who gives generously to all without finding fault, and it will be given to you. James 1: 5

The tongue has the power of life and death, and those who love it will eat its fruit. Prov. 18:21

...offer your bodies as a living sacrifice, holy and pleasing to God—this is your true and proper worship. 2 Do not conform to the pattern of this world, but be transformed by the renewing of your mind. Then you will be able to test and approve what God's will is—his good, pleasing and perfect will. Romans 12: 1-2

Scriptures to Think About

I can do all things through Christ who strengthens me. Philippians 4:13

For God hath not given us the spirit of fear, but of power, and of love, and of a sound mind. 2 Tim. 1:7

If we confess our sins, he is faithful and just and will forgive us our sins and purify us from all unrighteousness. 1 John 1:9

But to you who are listening I say: Love your enemies, do good to those who hate you, bless those who curse you, pray for those who mistreat you. Do to others as you would have them do to you. Luke 6: 27-28,31

...Everyone should be quick to listen, slow to speak and slow to become angry, because human anger does not produce the righteousness that God desires. James 1: 19-20

If any of you lacks wisdom, you should ask God, who gives generously to all without finding fault, and it will be given to you. James 1: 5

The tongue has the power of life and death, and those who love it will eat its fruit. Prov. 18:21

...offer your bodies as a living sacrifice, holy and pleasing to God—this is your true and proper worship. 2 Do not conform to the pattern of this world, but be transformed by the renewing of your mind. Then you will be able to test and approve what God's will is—his good, pleasing and perfect will. Romans 12: 1-2

MADE IN HIS IMAGE
Sessions 9-13

Theme Overview

The focus of this theme is to teach the girls that they are made in Christ's image, and that we should aim to "look" like Christ by the way we live our lives. Through an introduction to the Fruits of the Spirit, the girls will learn how having the "mind of Christ" is applied in everyday life. Through discussions on self-esteem, the girls will learn they are beautifully and wonderfully made in God's image. The lessons in this theme focus on living a righteous life and the importance of forgiveness, dealing with stress, worry, anger, and following Jesus' example of servant leadership.

Session 9

What's on Your Tree?

SESSION GOALS:

D.I.V.A. participants will:
- Learn about the Fruits of the Spirit–as visual characteristics of the Holy Spirit
- Examine themselves to reflect on the Fruits of the Spirit displayed in their personal lives
- Identify prayer focus areas to "shine a brighter light" for Christ

SCRIPTURE FOCUS:

Galatians 5:13-26; Galatians 5:22-25 (NLT); Luke 6:43-44 See also Luke 18:18-19; Psalm 28:7; Isaiah 26:3; 1 Corinthians 13: 1-8

MATERIALS NEEDED:

- D.I.V.A. Handbooks, one book for each girl
- Bibles: Inform the girls to bring Bibles if they have them
- "What's on Your Tree" Fruits of the Spirit signs (one of each sign)
- "What's on Your Tree" Worksheet (one for each girl)
- Pens (one for each girl)
- Tape

PREP TASKS:

- Print and post the "What's on Your Tree? signs around the room.
- Print "what's on your tree" worksheet for each girl.

RECALL (if applicable)

If applicable, follow the directions for facilitating the recall segment described in the introduction on page 18.

CHECK –IN

Make up your own Check-In activity or facilitate the "Highs and Lows" Check-In activity described in the introduction on page 17.

FOUNDATION

Share with the group:

Today we will discuss showing Christ-like traits in the way we live our lives.

Ask the girls, "Do you have any traits like your biological mother or father? (i.e. eyes, nose, sense of humor, etc.) Discuss their responses.

Share with the group:

Just like we have physical and personality traits that make us look or act like our parents, as children of God, we should also show characteristics that make us look like our Heavenly Father. When we accept Christ as our Lord and Savior, we receive the Holy Spirit, who lives inside of us (See sessions 2 and 5). Characteristics such as love, joy, peace, and self-control are evidence that God's spirit is inside of us. These are some of the traits people should see when they interact with us. These traits are called the Fruit of the Spirit.

Ask someone to read Galatians 5:13-26. Highlight the following scriptures providing the comments below each scripture.

Galatians 5:13-14
You, my brothers and sisters, were called to be free. But do not use your freedom to indulge the flesh; rather, serve one another humbly in love. For the entire law is fulfilled in keeping this one command: "Love your neighbor as yourself."

God is serious about showing love to others! This is the best way that we can show we are His children. All of the Fruits of the Spirit are focused on this command - to love others like we love ourselves.

Galatians 5:16-17
So I say, walk by the Spirit, and you will not gratify the desires of the flesh. For the flesh desires what is contrary to the Spirit, and the Spirit what is contrary to the flesh. They are in conflict with each other, so that you are not to do whatever you want.

Human nature will always cause us to want to do things that are against what God wants for us. This is temptation (See session 3). This is the constant struggle of every Christian. God is calling us to follow the guidance of His Holy Spirit within us, and this sometimes means we have to push what we want to the side and follow God.

Galatians 5:22-25 (NLT)
But the Holy Spirit produces this kind of fruit in our lives: love, joy, peace, patience, kindness, goodness, faithfulness, gentleness, and self-control. There is no law against these things! Those who belong to Christ Jesus have nailed the passions and desires of their sinful nature to his cross and crucified them there. Since we are living by the Spirit, let us follow the Spirit's leading in every part of our lives.

We belong to Christ, and not ourselves! And since we call ourselves children of God, we should act like we know Him!

Share with the group:

These traits are called "fruits" because they are produced in us through having a personal relationship with God.

Ask someone if they can share what the letter I stands for in the D.I.V.A. acronym (See session 1). Allow the group to respond first. Then remind them that the "I" stands for Integrity, which means "complete, undivided, and adhering to Christian values; committed to letting our words match our actions." Tell the girls that you will share a simple way to remember this. Ask everyone to raise their left and right hands in the air. Explain that the left hand represents what you say (i.e. I am a child of God) and the right hands represents what you do (i.e. actions and attitudes whether positive or negative). Share that when we put our hands together they should line up (illustrate this by putting one hand directly on the other so all your fingers line up). This means what we say should line up with what we do. Now, twist one of your hands so that the alignment of the hands is off, and share when what we say (i.e. I'm a child of God) does not line up with what we do we have an integrity issue that needs to be fixed. If this is left off track it can create confusion and a lot of drama in our lives.

Ask someone to read Luke 6:43-44
No good tree bears bad fruit, nor does a bad tree bear good fruit. Each tree is recognized by its own fruit. People do not pick figs from thorn-bushes, or grapes from briers.

Share with the group:

Just as you would not find oranges growing on an apple tree, we cannot expect these "fruits" to be produced in us if we are not putting the things of God in us such as prayer, reading God's word, spending time with other Christians (fellowship), etc. God wants us to live our lives with integrity. For the purpose of our activities today, we are going to imagine ourselves as trees and image that the Fruits of the Spirit are the fruits on our trees. We will do some exercises to think about what "fruits" are on our trees.

DISCUSSION

Ask one girl to stand by each one of the Fruits of the Spirit signs you have posted around the room. Have each of the girls read the sign they are standing by. After each girl reads her sign, discuss it with the group to make sure they understand. Ask the group to share real life experiences where they showed evidence of the particular "fruit" on the sign, or situations where they experienced other people showing that "fruit."

ACTIVITY: What's on Your Tree?

Distribute the "What's on Your Tree?" worksheet and pens. Give the girls about 10 minutes to complete the worksheet, filling out the three sections on the worksheet to reflect on what fruits are already on their tree (Positive and negative), what fruits need to fall off their tree (i.e. bad attitude, anger, etc.), and what seeds need to be planted (i.e. more patience). After they have completed the worksheet, ask the girls to stand by the "Fruit of the Spirit sign that represents an area they want to grow in. Discuss their responses and other entries on their worksheets.

D.I.V.A. CHALLENGE

Share with the group:

The D.I.V.A. Challenge for this week is to pray about the fruit that needs to fall off your tree, and make some concrete efforts this week in the areas where you need to plant new seeds. Write about it in your handbook.

Tell the girls you will ask them to report on their progress with this challenge at the next session.

CLOSING REFLECTION & PRAYER

Display the integrity illustration with your hands and share with the group:

As we grow closer in our relationship with God it will become easier for us to show these fruits when we interact with others. However, we will never get it 100% right; God knows this and still loves us in spite of this. Each day we should aim to live a life of integrity, so our fruits will show that we are God's children.

Invite a girl to pray out loud for the group based on the topic discussed. End the session with this prayer:

Father God, thank you so much for your faithfulness to us. Thank you for the gift of your Holy Spirit to transform us from the inside out. Help us show the Fruits of the Spirit to the world so that they may see you in us. Help us to keep your command to love others like we love ourselves. Thank you for your grace and mercy.

What's on Your Tree?

But the fruit of the Spirit is love, joy, peace, patience, kindness, goodness, faithfulness, gentleness and self-control. Against such things there is no law. – Galatians 5: 22-23 (NIV)

KINDNESS & GOODNESS

Striving to meet the standard God has set for us, and attempting to be righteous and follow Christ's example. Although none are good (Luke 18: 18-19), we strive every day to reach the expectations God has for us.

What's on Your Tree?

But the fruit of the Spirit is love, joy, peace, patience, kindness, goodness, faithfulness, gentleness and self-control. Against such things there is no law. – Galatians 5: 22-23 (NIV)

PATIENCE & SELF-CONTROL

Self-control means being slow to anger and able to control our desires when we are tempted. Patience is a form of self-control. Although our flesh is weak, we can do all things through Christ who strengthens us (Philippians 4:13). By developing self-control we can defeat temptations, overcome sin, grow in Christ, and show the fruits of the spirit in our life.

What's on Your Tree?

But the fruit of the Spirit is love, joy, peace, patience, kindness, goodness, faithfulness, gentleness and self-control. Against such things there is no law. – Galatians 5: 22-23 (NIV)

The joy of the Lord is our strength. It takes happiness to another level because it is not based on our current circumstances. True joy is experienced in the Lord's presence!

What's on Your Tree?

But the fruit of the Spirit is love, joy, peace, patience, kindness, goodness, faithfulness, gentleness and self-control. Against such things there is no law. – Galatians 5: 22-23 (NIV)

PEACE

A state of tranquility or quiet despite the "winds of life" trying to blow you down! Peace is freedom from disturbance and oppressive thoughts. Peace is promised to those who keep their minds focused on God. True peace is experienced in the presence of the Holy Spirit!

What's on Your Tree?

But the fruit of the Spirit is love, joy, peace, patience, kindness, goodness, faithfulness, gentleness and self-control. Against such things there is no law. – Galatians 5: 22-23 (NIV)

GENTLENESS

Being humble and not considering ourselves to high above others. We must realize that humility is required, and that God is in control. We practice self-control as needed, and learn when to "hold our peace."   Gentleness is not a weakness!

What's on Your Tree?

But the fruit of the Spirit is love, joy, peace, patience, kindness, goodness, faithfulness, gentleness and self-control. Against such things there is no law. – Galatians 5: 22-23 (NIV)

FAITHFULNESS

We are disciples of Christ, and committed to our Christian walk. We make all attempts to "stick with it," and stay true to God's Word. When we mess up (and we will!), God is just to forgive us and help us get back on the right track!

What's on Your Tree?

But the fruit of the Spirit is love, joy, peace, patience, kindness, goodness, faithfulness, gentleness and self-control. Against such things there is no law. – Galatians 5: 22-23 (NIV)

LOVE

Not a careless, passing emotion! Love is patient, love is kind. It does not envy, it does not boast, it is not proud. It does not dishonor others, it is not self-seeking, it is not easily angered, it keeps no record of wrongs. Love does not delight in evil but rejoices with the truth. It always protects, always trusts, always hopes, always perseveres. Love never fails. (1 Cor 13: 1-8)

Love requires sacrifice!

But the fruit of the Spirit is love, joy, peace, patience, kindness, good-ness, faithfulness, gentleness and self-control. Against such things there is no law. – Galatians 5: 22-23 (NIV)

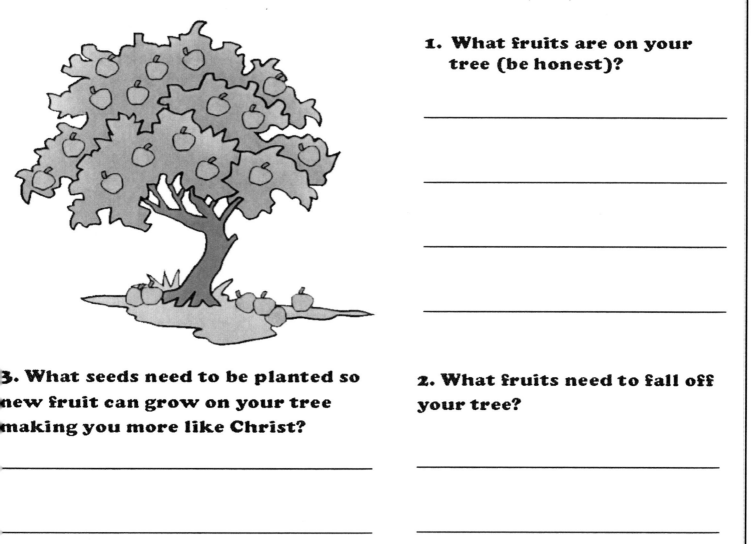

1. What fruits are on your tree (be honest)?

_____

_____

_____

_____

3. What seeds need to be planted so new fruit can grow on your tree making you more like Christ?

_____

_____

_____

_____

2. What fruits need to fall off your tree?

_____

_____

_____

_____

Session 10

New Eyes

SESSION GOALS:

D.I.V.A. participants will:
- Learn how self-esteem is formed
- Understand that we are all beautiful and made in God's image
- Hear God's perspective of us as revealed in scripture
- Discuss ways to boost our self-esteem

SCRIPTURE FOCUS:

Philippians 4:8; Proverbs 18:21 (NLT); Galatians 1:27; Psalm 139:13-15 (NLT) See also Jeremiah 29:11; Romans 8:37-38; Philippians 4:13; Isaiah 40:30-31

MATERIALS NEEDED:

- D.I.V.A. Handbooks, one book for each girl
- Bibles: Inform the girls to bring Bibles if they have them
- Markers
- Flip chart paper
- Enough play dough for each girl in the group to have some (This can be purchased from any Dollar store).
- Two different colors of Post-its (enough for each girl to have about 10 of each color)

PREP TASKS:

None

RECALL (if applicable)

If applicable, follow the directions for facilitating the recall segment described in the introduction on page 18.

CHECK –IN

Make up your own Check-In activity or facilitate the "Highs and Lows" Check-In activity described in the introduction on page 17.

FOUNDATION

Share with the group:

Today we will be discussing self-esteem.

Ask the group to define "Self-esteem," and discuss their responses.

Share with the group:

Self-esteem is simply your attitude towards and your view of yourself. You can have high or low self-esteem. Some of us may have experienced both at some time in our lives.

90

On the flip chart paper, draw a line down the middle. Write "low self-esteem" on one side of the line, and "high self-esteem" on the other. Ask the group, "What are common traits of people with high self-esteem/low self-esteem?" Write down their responses on the paper.

Ask the group, "What are things that affect our self-esteem? Where does our view of ourselves come from?" The girls may give some of the following responses: family, friends, media, failure, abuse, life experiences. Discuss their responses.

Share with the group:

All of the things you all have mentioned, both positive and negative, affect our self-esteem. Our self-esteem is connected to our brain and it is also connected to messages we have received about ourselves from the time we were young until now.

Ask someone to read Philippians 4:8

Finally, brothers and sisters, whatever is true, whatever is noble, whatever is right, whatever is pure, whatever is lovely, whatever is admirable—if anything is excellent or praiseworthy—think about such things.

Share with the group:

The brain is very powerful. Messages that go into our mind, affect our behavior, attitude, and feelings about the world and ourselves. If a person constantly receives negative messages about herself, she may eventually start to believe those messages, whether they are true or not. This is why God speaks to us

through the Bible about our minds, and gives us guidance on what type of messages He wants us to receive.

Ask someone to read Proverbs 18:21 (NLT)

The tongue can bring death or life; those who love to talk will reap the consequences.

Share with the group:

Words have power! The old nursery rhyme, "Sticks and stones may break my bones, but words can never hurt me" is just not true! Words can speak life or death. Low self-esteem is often caused by harsh words that have been spoken. We are going to do an activity to help us think about the messages, both positive and negative, that we have received that have helped to shape our self-esteem.

ACTIVITY: Brain Power

Distribute play dough to each of the girls and ask them to create a brain. Give them about 10 minutes to create their brains out of the play dough. Encourage them to be creative. After they have completed their brain models, distribute one color of the post-its to the girls. Tell them that this color represents positive messages they have been given about themselves. Only one message should be on each post-it. Tell them to write a message on each post it and place the messages around their brain on the table. Now, distribute the other color post-its. Tell them that this color represents negative messages they have been given about themselves. Only one negative message should be on each post-it.

Ask them if they have any observations about their brains and the messages that have been placed around them. For example, are there more positive than negative messages? Or vice versa? Discuss their responses.

Ask someone to read Genesis 1:27

So God created mankind in his own image, in the image of God he created them; male and female he created them.

Tell the group that you will read some of God's messages to His children, and as you read each message, tell them to place one of the post-its that represent a positive message around their brains.

Messages from God:
- I plan to take care of you and give you a good future (Jeremiah 29:11)
- I chose you (1 Peter 2:9)
- I've got your back (Romans 8:37-38)
- You can do anything you put your mind to do through me, according to my will (Philippians 4:13)
- I care about what happens to you. I'm with you all the way to the end. (Isaiah 40: 30-31)

Ask someone to read Psalm 139:13-15 (NLT)

You made all the delicate, inner parts of my body and knit me together in my mother's womb. Thank you for making me so wonderfully complex! Your workmanship is marvelous—how well I know it. You watched me as I was being formed in utter seclusion, as I was woven together in the dark of the womb.

Share with the group:

We were created in God's image, and that means that we are pretty special! He knew us and molded us when we were still in our mothers' bellies. At that time, He created us to be like Him. Despite the negative messages that others may give us, God provides so many positive messages about who we are and how much He loves us. God wants us to think on these things (refer again to Philippians 4:8) so we can see us as He sees us. He wants us to see that we were wonderfully made by the Master himself!

DISCUSSION

Based on the activity and the scriptures read, lead the girls in a discussion using the following prompts:

- How does it feel to know that you are so important to God, and that he made you to "look" like him?
- What does it mean to you to be "fearfully and wonderfully made"?
- What do you think the writer of Psalms 139:13-15 means when he says, "you created my inmost being"?
- What goes through your mind when you hear that God personally knit you together and formed your body?
- How does the knowledge of God's love change the way that you look at yourself?

Share with the group:

- *Here are some strategies we can use to boost our self-esteem.*
- Think about the great strengths and talents God has blessed you with when you want to be hard on yourself

92

- Words are powerful! Catch yourself saying / thinking something negative about yourself and replace it with something positive or one of the scriptures we discussed today
- Develop a sense of humor - don't take yourself so seriously!
- Pray and talk to God. Your Heavenly Father is always available
- Read your Bible, and reflect on the promises God has for us.
- Think about the progress you are making by following God. This may be reflected in your words, thoughts, feelings, or behavior.

D.I.V.A. CHALLENGE

Share with the group:

The D.I.V.A. Challenge for this week is to read the following scriptures, and pray to God to receive "New Eyes," so you can begin to see yourself as He sees you. Write about it in your handbook.

- *Jeremiah 29:11*
- *Romans 8:37-38*
- *Philippians 4:13*
- *Isaiah 40:30-31*

Tell the girls you will ask them to report on their progress with this challenge at the next session.

CLOSING REFLECTION & PRAYER

Share with the group:

Sometimes, because of different things we go through in life, our self-esteem can take a hit.

Although we may have ups and downs, we can take joy in knowing that God created each one of us to be unique and beautiful in our own special way. God wants us to know that He created us PERFECTLY! He created us just as He wants us to be. You are made in His perfect image. As we grow in our relationship with God, He gives us "New Eyes" so we can see ourselves as God sees us. With this new vision of ourselves, we can see the wonderful things about ourselves, as well as the areas we need to work on. We gain a healthy and realistic view of ourselves. And as we can see ourselves more through God's eyes, our self-esteem grows and we begin to realize how very special we are!

Invite a girl to pray out loud for the group based on the topic discussed. End the session with this prayer:

Lord Jesus, thank you for your Holy Spirit. Thank you for your sacrifice, because through your death and resurrection we already have the victory over low self-esteem. Help us to read your Word and to pray more so we can begin to understand more about your love for us. Give us your eyes so we may see ourselves the way that you see us. Thank you for transforming us from the inside out to be used for your glory.

Session 11
Seventy Times Seven?!?!

SESSION GOALS:

D.I.V.A. participants will:
- Recognize God's divine forgiveness in our lives
- Learn that God requires us to forgive others in order to be forgiven by Him
- Learn the benefits of forgiveness

SCRIPTURE FOCUS:

John 3:16; Matthew 18:21-22 (NLT); 1 John 2:3-6; Luke 17:3-4 (MESSAGE); Matthew 7:1-2; Matthew 6:14-15

MATERIALS NEEDED:

- D.I.V.A. Handbooks, one book for each girl
- Bibles: Inform the girls to bring Bibles if they have them Markers
- Flip chart Paper
- Paper plates (one per girl)
- Sand (Enough for each girl to have some on her plate – can be found in the home décor section of a dollar store or craft store)

PREP TASKS:

None

RECALL (if applicable)

If applicable, follow the directions for facilitating the recall segment described in the introduction on page 18.

CHECK –IN

Make up your own Check-In activity or facilitate the "Highs and Lows" Check-In activity described in the introduction on page 17.

FOUNDATION

Share with the group:
Today we will be talking about forgiveness—both how God forgives us and how he requires us to forgive others.

Ask someone to read John 3:16
For God so loved the world that he gave his one and only Son, that whoever

believes in him shall not perish but have eternal life.

Share with the group:

God's relationship with us is the ultimate example of how we should forgive. He sent His son, Jesus, to die on the cross for our sins. When He died on the cross, Jesus took our place and saved us from having to suffer the horrible consequences of our sin. Despite this, we often live our lives as if Jesus did not give His life for us. We constantly act in ways that do not allow us to shine our light for Christ. Even though we go against His directions for how to live our lives, He still forgives us over and over because He loves us.

Ask the group, "Has anyone ever held a grudge?" Discuss some of the reasons they have held a grudge. Ask if anyone has had other people hold a grudge against them. If someone answers yes, ask them how it made them feel. Discuss their responses.

Ask someone to read Matthew 18:21-22 (NLT)

Then Peter came to him and asked, "Lord, how often should I forgive someone who sins against me? Seven times?" "No, not seven times," Jesus replied, "but seventy times seven!

Ask the group for their responses to this scripture. Discuss their responses.

Share with the group:

If we do the math, this adds up to 490 times! Now, does this mean we have to forgive others up to 490 times before we can hold a grudge? Not! Jesus doesn't want us to get caught up in the numbers. The bigger message is that as many times as someone offends us, we should forgive them. Just as Jesus forgives us each time we ask. Wow, that's a hard pill to swallow. Sometimes it can be so hard to forgive because people have hurt us so bad. Usually, it's the people that we love the most that do the most damage--- our family and friends.

Ask the girls to share some of the deepest hurts they have suffered that have made it hard to forgive at different times of their lives. As they share, try to summarize the major offenses (i.e. betrayal, deception, abandonment, humiliation, etc.) that the girls suffered and write them on the flip chart paper. Discuss their perceptions of why it's hard to forgive in these instances.

Read Luke 17:3-4 (The Message)
"Be alert. If you see your friend going wrong, correct him. If he responds, forgive him. Even if it's personal against you and repeated seven times through the day, and seven times he says, 'I'm sorry, I won't do it again,' forgive him."

Share with the group:

I don't know about you all, but it sounds like this scripture is talking about me. I can't count the number of times I've said "I'm sorry, I won't do it again" to God only to turn around and do that same thing again. This scripture is showing us that us forgiving other people is supposed to mirror God forgiving us. How powerful!

Ask someone to read the following scriptures:

Matthew 6:14-15
For if you forgive other people when they sin against you, your heavenly Father will also forgive you. But if you do not forgive others their sins, your Father will not forgive your sins.

Matthew 7:1-2
Do not judge, or you too will be judged. For in the same way you judge others, you will be judged, and with the measure you use, it will be measured to you.

Share with the group:

How Powerful! Our forgiveness of others is tied to the forgiveness we desperately need to receive from God. You see, asking for forgiveness is a cleansing exercise. Even if the person does not honor the forgiveness you have given, the act of forgiving them is not for them, it's for you! Holding on to unforgiveness can drive a wall between you and God because it is a symptom of pride. The Bible tells us that pride is a sin and it leads to us messing up. We cannot get closer to God if we have pride. Forgiving others brings us closer to God. It is more about obedience to Him than proving something to the other person.

ACTIVITY: Clean Slate

Distribute a paper plate to each girl, and pour some sand on each plate. Pour enough sand to fully cover a good portion of the plate. Instruct the girls to spread out, so that others can't see what they write. Ask the girls to first think of things they need to confess and repent for, and then instruct them to take their finger and write a word that describes it in their sand. They should not share these things out loud with the group. Tell them to take a moment of silence and ask God for forgiveness. Once they have repented, tell them to gently shake their paper plate so that the sand moves and clears the word from their plate. This process can be repeated a few times if desired.

Now, ask them to write a word in their sand for something that they need to forgive someone else for. Tell them to take a moment of silence and ask God to help them to forgive. Once they have silently prayed, tell them to gently shake their paper plate so that the sand moves and clears the word from their plate. This process can be repeated a few times if desired.

Read 1 John 2:3-6
We know that we have come to know him if we keep his commands. Whoever says, "I know him," but does not do what he commands is a liar, and the truth is not in that person. But if anyone obeys his word, love for God is truly made complete in them. This is how we know we are in him: Whoever claims to live in him must live as Jesus did.

Share with the group:

This is a clear way of showing how God wipes the slate clean when we ask for forgiveness. Jesus is our ultimate example. We should follow His example in forgiving others. It is a way to show others the love God shows for us time and time again. Forgiving others allows us to grow closer to Him and to grow stronger in our faith.

Discussion

Based on the activity and the scriptures read, lead the girls in a discussion using the following prompts:

- With this new information, does it make it any easier to forgive others? Why or Why not?
- Is there a particular offense done to you that you need to "erase in the sand?"
- Do you have any new insights of awareness about God's forgiveness towards us? If so, what have you learned?
- Have you learned anything about yourself from this lesson? If so, what have you learned?
- In what ways can you use this information when you leave today?

D.I.V.A. Challenge

Share with the group:

The D.I.V.A. Challenge for this week is to start the process of forgiving someone else by writing a letter to someone who has hurt you. In the letter, describe what upset you and how it made you feel. Share with them what you have learned about forgiveness through God forgiving you. Pray about what you write in the letter to ask God to help you to truly forgive that person. It is not required, but if you feel the need to, share the letter with the person or talk to the person about your letter. Write about it in your handbook.

Tell the girls you will ask them to report on their progress with this challenge at the next session.

Closing Reflection & Prayer

Share with the group:

It can be very difficult to forgive others at times, but Jesus is our ultimate example. His death on the cross for our sins, overcame everything that would ever try to separate us from Him. He forgives us daily for our sins, and His love for us gives us the strength to forgive others.

Invite a girl to pray out loud for the group based on the topic discussed. End the session with this prayer:

Father God, thank you for loving us. Forgive us for things we have done and said that did not bring glory to you. Help us to truly repent and turn away from those things. Thank you for forgiving us over and over again and wiping our slates clean. Heal us from the hurts that others have done to us, and help us to follow your lead by truly forgiving them. Help us to show others the love you have shown to us.

Session 12

Seeing Red

SESSION GOALS:

D.I.V.A. participants will:
- Understand that anger is a natural emotion
- Review biblical perspectives on handling anger
- Learn to follow Jesus' example when dealing with anger

SCRIPTURE FOCUS:

Ephesians 4:26-27 (The Message); James 1:19-21; Ecclesiastes 7:9 (NLT); Proverbs 19:11 (NLT); Romans 12:17-19 (The Message); Proverbs 15:18 (The Message)

MATERIALS NEEDED:

- D.I.V.A. Handbooks, one book for each girl
- Bibles: Inform the girls to bring Bibles if they have them
- Red marker
- Flip Chart paper
- Seeing Red, Role Play Scenarios (one copy for each group of 3-4 girls)

PREP TASKS:

- Recreate the "Seeing Red Scale" (located at the end of this session) on the flip chart paper using the red marker.
- Prepare another sheet of flip chart paper with "ANGER: What Happens…" across the top with three columns under it. Label the columns "Physically," "Emotionally," and "Spiritually."

RECALL (if applicable)

If applicable, follow the directions for facilitating the recall segment described in the introduction on page 18.

CHECK –IN

Make up your own Check-In activity or facilitate the "Highs and Lows" Check-In activity described in the introduction on page 17.

FOUNDATION

Share with the group:

Today we will be talking about anger, and how we should deal with our anger so we still shine our lights for Christ. Anger is a natural emotion that we experience when things don't go the way we think they should. Anger can be mild like being annoyed, or extreme like being in a rage. Even God gets angry. Remember we are made in His image. Getting angry is not the problem. How we handle our anger is what most often leads to problems.

Using the "Seeing Red Scale" you have created on the flip chart paper, ask the girls what makes them angry. Ask them about the level of anger (mild, moderate, severe) and write the issue under the appropriate section of the scale. Then ask the girls, how they deal with the anger. Write their answers on the sheet and discuss their responses.

Share with the group:

Not handling our anger in the right way, opens us up to sin and dishonoring ourselves and God in many ways. This may include engaging in violent behavior, becoming depressed, using foul language, and many other issues. Remember, we belong to God, so we want to try our best to represent Him at all times with our words and our actions. It is important for us to understand what triggers our anger, and to pay attention to ourselves for warnings of when anger is starting to overwhelm us.

Using the "Anger: What happens..." sheet you have created, ask the group what begins to happen in their minds and bodies when anger develops. Allow the girls to respond first, and insert these major points where necessary:

Some physical responses that may occur as soon as you are angry (also known as "fight or flight"):

- Adrenaline starts pumping (boost of energy)
- Breathing speeds up
- Heart starts pounding
- Blood pressure increases and blood rushes to muscles, which causes some parts of the body to feel warm and tingly
- Muscles start to tense up in the face and rest of the body

Some emotional responses that may occur over time if anger is not handled properly:

- Depression
- Harmful behaviors (cutting, drug abuse, promiscuousness, poor eating habits, etc.)
- Nervousness
- Hard time focusing
- Feeling hurt, not valued, and/or disrespected (low self-esteem)
- Bitterness

Some spiritual responses that may occur over time if anger is not handled properly:

- We don't forgive, which makes it hard for us to receive God's forgiveness (See session 11)
- Stubbornness and pride develop that can put a wall between us and God

Designate girls to each read one of the following scriptures:

Ephesians 4:26-27 (The Message)
Go ahead and be angry. You do well to be angry—but don't use your anger as fuel for revenge. And don't stay angry. Don't go to bed angry. Don't give the Devil that kind of foothold in your life.

James 1:19-20
My dear brothers and sisters, take note of this: Everyone should be quick to listen, slow to speak and slow to become angry, because human anger does not produce the righteousness that God desires.

Ecclesiastes 7:9 (NLT)
Control your temper, for anger labels you a fool.

Proverbs 19:11 (NLT)
Sensible people control their temper; they earn respect by overlooking wrongs.

Romans 12:17-19 (The Message)
Don't hit back; discover beauty in everyone. If you've got it in you, get along with everybody. Don't insist on getting even; that's not for you to do. "I'll do the judging," says God. "I'll take care of it."

Proverbs 15:18 (The Message)
Hot tempers start fights; a calm, cool spirit keeps the peace.

Share with the group:

As we can see, anger if not handled the right way can cause a lot of problems and be downright dangerous! We must pick our battles and know when to let God fight for us. We have to figure out a productive way to use our angry energy.

ACTIVITY: How Do You Deal?

Divide the girls into groups of 3-4. Distribute the "How Do You Deal?" activity sheet. Assign the groups to a scenario. You can give more than one scenario to the groups if you have some scenarios left over. In each scenario the character has made a snap judgment of how to deal with the situation. Tell the girls to read the scenario as a group, discuss it, and determine a scripture at the bottom of the page that would be useful for the character in the scenario to read. Then, each group should develop a brief 1-2 minute role play to illustrate a healthier way the character can deal with her anger in the scenario. Allow the groups about 10-15 minutes to discuss and prepare their 1-2 minute role play. Each group should then present their role play to the larger group.

DISCUSSION

Discuss the scenarios and the healthier anger management strategies the groups displayed in their role plays. Based on the activity and the scriptures read, lead the girls in a discussion using the following prompts:

- Why do you think it is so hard for some people to choose to do some of the healthier alternatives you displayed in your role plays?
- What are some of the consequences of anger that you have experienced?
- What makes you the angriest? (These are called stressors.)

- How can you start to control your anger in these areas when issues arise?
- Do you have any new insights on the connection between controlling your anger and your personal relationship with God?

Share with the group:

Here are some strategies we can use to manage our anger:
- Prayer for wisdom, self-control, and the "mind of Christ"
- Pay attention-Be aware of your stressors and triggers so you can avoid them if possible
- Relax and breathe when a tough situation pops up to give yourself an opportunity to think
- Choose your battles-everything is not worth making a big fuss about!
- Try to change the way you think about it – Is there a different perspective to look at the issue that may help you figure out a better way to handle it?
- Change your environment – perhaps it's the people you are with or the places you are in
- Use the problem solving skills learned in Session 8
- Talk it out – with a trusted friend or adult
- Write it out – Express how you feel by journaling about it to release your thoughts
- Do something creative to get rid of the negative energy – music, dance, art, exercise, etc.

D.I.V.A. CHALLENGE

Share with the group:

The D.I.V.A. Challenge for this week is to think about a recent situation in which you let your anger get the best of you. Reread the scriptures from this lesson, and think about how you may have handled that situation in a more Godly way. Write about it in your handbook.

Tell the girls you will ask them to report on their progress with this challenge at the next session.

CLOSING REFLECTION & PRAYER

Share with the group:

Anger is a natural emotion, and God gives us wisdom and self-control to be able to manage it properly.

Invite a girl to pray out loud for the group based on the topic discussed. End the session with this prayer:

Merciful God, thank you for opening our eyes to how to live a life for you according to your Word. Forgive us for when we have let our anger get the best of us. Help us to recognize our triggers and when we are tempted to act out in anger in ways that don't honor you. If there is hurt and pain hidden under our anger, please heal us and make us whole. Thank you for self-control and wisdom. Help us to use these gifts when we are angry.

How angry are you?

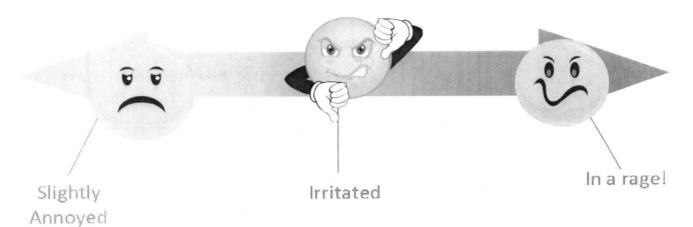

Slightly
Annoyed

Irritated

In a rage!

What makes you this angry?	What makes you this angry?	What makes you this angry?

How do you deal?

Session 13

Follow the Leader

SESSION GOALS:

D.I.V.A. participants will:

- Learn about Jesus' example of servant leadership
- Discuss the qualities of leadership according to biblical principles
- Assess their own leadership potential as children of God

SCRIPTURE FOCUS:

Titus 1: 5-9 (Message); Matthew 18:1-4; Luke 22:24-26 (Message);

See also Galatians 1:10; Philippians 2:3-4; Philippians 4:11-13; Colossians 3:22-23; Luke 16:10; John 13:1-17

MATERIALS NEEDED:

- D.I.V.A. Handbooks, one book for each girl
- Bibles: Inform the girls to bring Bibles if they have them
- Flip chart paper
- Markers
- Serving it Up! Activity Sheet (a copy for each girl)

PREP TASKS:

- Make a copy of the "Serving it Up!" activity sheet for each girl.

RECALL (if applicable)

If applicable, follow the directions for facilitating the recall segment described in the introduction on page 18.

CHECK –IN

Make up your own Check-In activity or facilitate the "Highs and Lows" Check-In activity described in the introduction on page 17.

FOUNDATION

Share with the group:

Today we will discuss what it means to be a leader. There are many definitions of leadership, but we will look at the example

Jesus sets for us to determine what it means to be a leader according to God's Word.

Ask the group, "What comes to your mind when you think of leadership?" Encourage them to brainstorm and think of all character traits and adjectives (not people) that come to mind. Write down their responses on the flip chart paper. After all ideas have been shared, go over the list and as a group, put a plus or minus sign next to each word to indicate if they believe the words have a positive or negative connotation. Discuss their responses.

Ask the girls to name people that exhibit the traits on the leadership list they have come up with. These may include adults in their lives, peers, family members, media personalities, and/or themselves. Write their responses on another sheet of paper.

Now that the group has had some discussion about leadership, ask them to come up with a simple definition of leadership based on the discussion. Write their definition on another sheet of the flip chart paper. Post all three sheets in a visible location in the room. The group will return to these sheets throughout the session.

Share with the group:

Now that we have discussed our ideas about leadership, let's see what the Bible says about it. Then we can compare how our thoughts about leadership line up with God's thoughts about it.

Take a blank sheet and write "What the Bible says" on it. Inform the girls, that as you read the scriptures, we will add characteristics to this list to show what the Bible says about

leadership. Enlist a volunteer to add words to the board as the group learns biblical leadership traits throughout the session.

Distribute the following scriptures to a few girls for them to read, and share the comments in between the scriptures:

Titus 1:5-9 (The Message)
I left you in charge in Crete so you could complete what I left half-done. Appoint leaders in every town according to my instructions. As you select them, ask, "Is this man well-thought-of? Is he committed to his wife? Are his children believers? Do they respect him and stay out of trouble?" It's important that a church leader, responsible for the affairs in God's house, be looked up to—not pushy, not short-tempered, not a drunk, not a bully, not money-hungry. He must welcome people, be helpful, wise, fair, reverent, have a good grip on himself, and have a good grip on the Message, knowing how to use the truth to either spur people on in knowledge or stop them in their tracks if they oppose it.

Ask the girls; what words can be pulled from this scripture to describe leaders. Assist them with locating leadership characteristics in the scripture. Target words include: good reputation, wise, role model, respects God, self-control, integrity (practice what you preach), know God's Word, use God's Word to help people become better. Ask the volunteer to add these words to the "What the Bible says" list.

Share with the group:

In other translations, this passage includes the word "blameless." "Blameless" does not mean that you are perfect or without sin, because we all sin. That's why we need Jesus! Being blameless means that your intentions are pure, and that you have a reputation for trying to live for God with everything you have. Due to this, the scriptures are saying, that it will be hard for others to criticize you or accuse you of something bad because of the example you have shown.

Ask the volunteer to add blameless to the "What the Bible says" list.

Matthew 18:1-4
At that time the disciples came to Jesus and asked, "Who, then, is the greatest in the kingdom of heaven?" He called a little child to him, and placed the child among them. And he said: "Truly I tell you, unless you change and become like little children, you will never enter the kingdom of heaven. Therefore, whoever takes the lowly position of this child is the greatest in the kingdom of heaven.

Ask the girls; what words can be pulled from this scripture to describe leaders. Assist them with locating leadership characteristics in the scripture. Target words include: humility, faith. Ask the volunteer to add these words to the "What the Bible says" list.

Luke 22:24-26 (The Message)
Within minutes they were bickering over who of them would end up the greatest. But Jesus intervened: "Kings like to throw their weight around and people in authority like to give themselves fancy titles. It's not going to be that way with you. Let the senior among you become like the junior; let the leader act the part of the servant.

Ask the girls; what words can be pulled from this scripture to describe leaders. Assist them with locating leadership characteristics in the scripture. Target words include: humility, servant. Ask the volunteer to add these words to the "What the Bible says" list.

Share with the group:

There are a lot of similarities between the world's definition of leadership and God's definition of leadership. However, the main thing that really stands out about God's definition is that leadership is about service. It's more about the people you serve than it is about you. It is not about fame and power, but about using your life to help other people find Christ and live their lives for him. Jesus is our ultimate example. He served us by dying for our sins. He serves us by loving us, protecting us, and guiding us each day through our lives. God is calling us to be leaders by serving others and helping them find their way to Him.

ACTIVITY: Serving it Up!

Inform the girls that they will do an activity to learn more words to add to the "What the Bible Says" list. Divide the girls into five small groups and distribute the "Serving it up!" activity sheet titled, "Qualities of a Servant Leader." Assign each group a scripture from the sheet. Instruct them to find the scripture in their Bibles, read the scripture as a group, discuss the leadership traits within it, and come up with a creative way to present the scripture and the leadership traits within it back to the large group. Walk around and assist the groups with identifying the leadership traits if needed. Their presentation can take the form of a poem, rap, skit, commercial, cheer/chant, nursery rhyme, children's story, etc. The more creative the better! After each group presents back to the large group, add the leadership traits from their presentation to the "What the Bible Says" list.

Key Leadership Traits:

1. Galatians 1:10 - God Comes First. People are important, but pleasing God comes first. Sometimes people won't like God's plan for our lives, but we have to do His will first.

2. Philippians 2:3-4 – They consider other people. God does not want us to be self-centered and only consider our own needs. Putting others first is a true characteristic of a servant leader.

3. Philippians 4:11-13 – They are thankful for their blessings. Servant leaders try to not take things for granted and serve others without complaining.

4. Colossians 3:22-23 – They are hard workers. Servant leaders give 100%, not half-hearted efforts. They realize they are really working for God so they follow through and give their all.

5. Luke 16:10 – They are trustworthy. Service should be done with faithfulness. If we agree to help someone or do something, we need to follow through with it.

DISCUSSION

Compare the list the group created with the "What the Bible Says" list. Compare and discuss the lists with the girls using the following prompts:
- What are the similarities on the two lists?
- Is there anything that doesn't match up on our lists?
- Did we forget anything on our list that was on the Bible list? If so, why do you think we overlooked that?
- Do you know anyone that shows the characteristics on the Bible list, in the way they live their lives?
- What type of people do you think can be leaders based on the Bible list?

Then, ask the girls to reflect on their own leadership example based on the Bible list. Lead the girls in a discussion using the following prompts:
- Do you consider yourself a leader? Why or Why not?
- In what ways are you a leader? (i.e. in school or church? Amongst family and friends?)
  - Who looks to your example?
  - How can you be a servant in these leadership roles?
- What traits on the Bible list do you show as a leader?
- As a child of God, what areas would you like to improve in to better show your leadership skills?
- With all that we learned today, what can you take away as your personal definition of leadership?

D.I.V.A. CHALLENGE

Share with the group:

The D.I.V.A. Challenge for this week is to read John 13:1-17, a story about Jesus serving His disciples. Read the passage and think about what you can learn from Jesus' example of being a servant leader. Think about how you

106

can apply the information you gather from it to your life. Write about it in your handbook.

Tell the girls you will ask them to report on their progress with this challenge at the next session.

CLOSING REFLECTION & PRAYER

Share with the group:

Based on scripture, our life experiences, and our discussions today, we can all probably expand our definition of leadership. Leadership is about knowing who we are as God's children, and that He created each of us for a special purpose. Leadership is about serving others. God can use anybody, regardless of if we are the "typical" leader or not. God calls all of us to be leaders in some area in our lives. We can be certain that just by choosing to live for God we have chosen to be leaders. We show leadership by showing others Christ in us through living a life of service, and displaying His love in our words and actions.

Invite a girl to pray out loud for the group based on the topic discussed. End the session with this prayer:

Lord Jesus, thank you for your wonderful example of servant leadership. Help us to follow in your foot steps to serve others in love, just as you serve us. Where there is pride, arrogance, laziness, or self-doubt, remove those things from us so we can go forward boldly in knowing that you have created all of us to be leaders for you. Help us to remember to give you the glory for all that you will do through us.

Qualities of a Servant Leader

Group 1 Scripture: Galatians 1:10
Qualities of a Servant Leader:

Presentation Ideas:

Group 2 Scripture: Philippians 2:3-4
Qualities of a Servant Leader:

Presentation Ideas:

Group 3 Scripture: Philippians 4:11-13
Qualities of a Servant Leader:

Presentation Ideas:

Group 4 Scripture: Colossians 3: 22-23
Qualities of a Servant Leader:

Presentation Ideas:

Group 5 Scripture: Luke 16:10
Qualities of a Servant Leader:

Presentation Ideas:

MY BODY IS A TEMPLE
Sessions 14-17

Theme Overview:

This theme centers on treating our bodies as temples of God. A central key scripture for all the sessions in this theme is 1 Corinthians 6:19-20:

Do you not know that your bodies are temples of the Holy Spirit, who is in you, whom you have received from God? You are not your own; you were bought at a price. Therefore honor God with your bodies.

Through these sessions, girls are encouraged to think of their bodies, in physical and spiritual contexts, as a home for God's Holy Spirit. Through lessons on body image, personal hygiene, dealing with sexual temptation, and media consumption; the girls will learn that they are fearfully and wonderfully made to give God glory in all parts of their lives. Above all, through continuing to learn about God in the context of group fellowship and support, the girls will learn that they were bought with a price that we must honor God with our bodies.

Session 14

Looking in the Mirror

SESSION GOALS:

D.I.V.A. participants will:
- Understand body image
- Discuss their feelings about their bodies and physical appearance
- Learn that our perception of our bodies determine how we care for them
- Understand the connection between body image and our personal relationship with God

SCRIPTURE FOCUS:

Proverbs 31:30 (NLT), Psalm 139:13-16 (NLT)

MATERIALS NEEDED:

- D.I.V.A. Handbooks, one book for each girl
- Bibles: Inform the girls to bring Bibles if they have them
- Flip chart paper
- Banner paper (Need enough for each girl to trace her body outline)
- Scissors
- 11x14 size poster board (or similar size) for each girl.
- Markers
- Tape
- Large Mirror (portable or the mirror in nearby room)
- Window Paint Markers (Available at most office supply stores)
- Old towel (to wipe off window paint markers)

PREP TASKS:

None

RECALL (if applicable)

If applicable, follow the directions for facilitating the recall segment described in the introduction on page 18.

CHECK –IN

Make up your own Check-In activity or facilitate the "Highs and Lows" Check-In activity described in the introduction on page 17.

FOUNDATION

Share with the group:

Many girls struggle with their self-esteem because of their physical appearance. God has made each of us beautiful in our own way, both inside and out. Today we will share and discuss our thoughts and feelings about our bodies and physical appearance.

Ask the group, "What is body image?" Discuss their responses.

Share with the group:

Your body image is how you feel about your body and your physical appearance. You can have a positive or negative body image. Over time, we may find ourselves having a positive body image at one point and a negative body image at another. This may depend on what is going on in our lives at the time.

Ask the girls to brainstorm descriptions for positive and negative body image. Write down their responses on the flip chart paper. Discuss their responses, and add the following points to the discussion.

- ✓ Positive Body Image
  - Appreciate and celebrate your natural body shape
  - Understand that a person's physical appearance is only a part of who they are and that physical appearance says little about their character or value as a person
  - Have a clear perception of your shape-you see your body as it really is and feel comfortable in it

- ✓ Negative Body Image
  - Have a distorted perception of your shape—you see your body differently than it actually is
  - Think other people find you unattractive, when that may not be the case

- See your size or shape as a sign of personal failure
- Feel uncomfortable in your own body
- Feel ashamed, self-conscious and anxious about your body

Ask for volunteers to read the following scriptures. Discuss with the group their thoughts on the connection between body image and the scriptures as you read them.

Psalm 139:13-16 (NLT)
You made all the delicate, inner parts of my body and knit me together in my mother's womb. Thank you for making me so wonderfully complex! Your workmanship is marvelous—how well I know it. You watched me as I was being formed in utter seclusion, as I was woven together in the dark of the womb. You saw me before I was born. Every day of my life was recorded in your book. Every moment was laid out before a single day had passed. How precious are your thoughts about me, O God. They cannot be numbered!

Proverbs 31:30 (NLT)
Charm is deceptive, and beauty does not last; but a woman who fears the Lord will be greatly praised.

Share with the group:

Body image is all about your perception of yourself. Having a positive body image does not mean that you like everything about your body because there may be some steps we need to take to be healthier, such as eating better and exercising. However, a positive body image means that you realize that your physical body, despite its flaws, is a gift from

God and a home for His Holy Spirit. It means that you are realistic about your body, including any healthy lifestyle choices you want to make. It means that you realize that your physical appearance is just one part of you, and that other parts of you like your mind, your personality, and your attempts to "look" like Christ make you beautiful too. If left unchecked, having a negative body image can cause you to obsess about your body, which can lead to unhealthy behaviors like unhealthy amounts of exercise, poor eating habits, and low self-esteem. It could even lead to more extreme unhealthy behaviors including eating disorders, depression, and even drug use. It is very important that we develop a healthy and positive relationship with our bodies!

ACTIVITY: Body Beautiful

Inform the girls that they will do an activity to think about their own body image and the outside influences on their perception of themselves. Help each girl get a sheet of banner paper that is approximately her height. (They may also tape several sheets of flip chart paper together for this activity.) Instruct the girls to work together to trace their body outlines on their papers. Give each girl two different color markers. Tell them to follow the instructions, and give them the following prompts:

- On the INSIDE of their body outlines, tell them to write everything they like about their bodies in one of the colors. They can do this using words or by drawing pictures.

- On the INSIDE of their body outlines, tell them to write everything they don't like about their bodies in the other color. They can do this using words or by drawing pictures.

- On the OUTSIDE of their body outlines, tell them to write the influences on how they feel about their bodies. "Where do these thoughts come from? " Responses may include family, friends, boys, media, etc.

- Tell them to circle the words/pictures they feel they can control. For example, "being overweight" is something that can be controlled through diet and exercise, but "shoe size" is out of one's control.

- Tell them they can decorate their pictures if they would like to.

Once the girls are finished with their pictures, have them present their pictures back to the large group. Share your thoughts with the group on any commonalities among the pictures, or anything that stands out to you. Ask the girls to share their thoughts on these points as well.

DISCUSSION

Based on the activity and the scriptures read, lead the girls in a discussion using the following prompts:
- What are your thoughts about the words you circled on your paper? What are your thoughts about the words that you did not circle on your paper?

- Do you think body image problems are a major issue for most girls? If so, why?

- How can we turn unhealthy behaviors, that may be negatively affecting our body image (i.e. putting ourselves down, poor eating habits, etc.), into healthy behaviors to give our body image a boost?

- What are some strategies we can use to combat the negative messages we receive about our bodies?

- What's one thing you can do differently to help you think about your body as God's temple?

- In your opinion, what does our body image have to do with our personal relationship with God?

ACTIVITY: Mirror, Mirror

Take out the large mirror(s) or take the girls to a nearby room with a mirror. Distribute the window markers.

Share with the group:

Our prayer is that we can begin to see ourselves as God sees us, and if there are changes we need to make, that God will give us the strength and wisdom to do so. God made each one of us to be beautiful and unique in our own way. As the scriptures tell us, we are "fearfully and wonderfully" made, God's masterpiece! Look in the mirror, and write something on the mirror that you think is beautiful about yourself. Say it out loud, and then write it on the mirror. This can be

something about your body or your personality.

Give the girls time to write their words down. If a girl is having a hard time with the exercise, invite the group to share beautiful characteristics about that person. If the group is not mature enough to do this, the leader should share a characteristic about that person. After the closing reflection and prayer, have the girls to wipe the mirror with a damp towel to remove the window marker.

Share with the group:

Don't put yourself down if there are things about yourself you don't like. Instead, get a plan together to help you make reasonable changes to be healthier. Enlist a trusted adult to help you put your plan together.

D.I.V.A. CHALLENGE

Distribute the poster boards to each girl.

Share with the group:

This week the D.I.V.A. Challenge is to create a collage, using words and images from old magazines, that communicates positive messages to girls about their bodies and what God's Word says to us. Pick one of the scriptures shared today (Proverbs 31:30 or Psalm 139:13-16) as your theme scripture to inspire your collage. Write about it in your handbook.

Tell the girls to bring their collages to share at the next session. If the group has a dedicated meeting space, hang their collages up as room decorations and reminders of God's love for us.

CLOSING REFLECTION & PRAYER

Share with the group:

We come in many sizes, and with many areas that we both like and dislike about our bodies. We can make changes about some of these areas, and some of them we cannot. How we view our bodies determines how we care for our bodies. Regardless of whatever challenges we face with our body image, God loves us despite our flaws. If there are things we need to change, He will help us to do so. If we have an unrealistic view of our bodies, we can pray for God to adjust our vision of ourselves. The main point of this session is for us to realize that God loves us and He wants us to love our bodies!

Invite a girl to pray out loud for the group based on the topic discussed. End the session with this prayer:

Awesome God, thank you for this lesson. Thank you for health and for your gift of life. You are such a gracious God. Help us to develop a healthy image of ourselves that aligns with how you see us. Help us to love and take care of our bodies, understanding that they are a dwelling place for your Holy Spirit. If any negative perceptions or dangerous behaviors exist among us, wash us clean with your love and the cleansing blood already shed through Jesus Christ. Thank you for making us whole.

Session 15

So Fresh & So Clean

SESSION GOALS:

D.I.V.A. participants will:
- Learn about personal hygiene concepts (menstruation, skin care, hair care, and dental care)
- Understand the connection between personal hygiene and our bodies as temples of the Lord

SCRIPTURE FOCUS:

Romans 12:1-2; Colossians 3:17

MATERIALS NEEDED:
- D.I.V.A. Handbooks, one book for each girl
- Bibles: Inform the girls to bring Bibles if they have them
- "So Fresh & So Clean" Handout
- Flip chart paper or Dry Erase Board
- Markers/Dry Erase Markers
- Dry Eraser (if applicable)
- Inexpensive prizes for the winning Jeopardy game team. (Great options that go with this are items that go with the session theme such as mini shower gels, hand lotion, nail polish, lip gloss, etc.)

PREP TASKS:
- Make a copy of the "So Fresh & So Clean" handout for each girl
- Create Jeopardy game board detailed in the activity section of the session

----

RECALL (if applicable)

If applicable, follow the directions for facilitating the recall segment described in the introduction on page 18.

CHECK –IN

Make up your own Check-In activity or facilitate the "Highs and Lows" Check-In activity described in the introduction on page 17.

FOUNDATION

Share with the group:

From the "tween" years and up through the teen years, there are a lot of changes happening in our bodies. From our first menstrual cycle, to changes in our skin, hair,

115

and teeth, women have a lot to deal with! Today we will discuss the importance of taking care of our bodies.

Ask the group, "What are some personal hygiene strategies you use to take care of your body?" Responses may include daily shower/bath, getting a manicure/pedicure, washing hair once a week, etc. Discuss their responses.

Ask someone to read the following scriptures:

Romans 12:1-2
Therefore, I urge you, brothers and sisters, in view of God's mercy, to offer your bodies as a living sacrifice, holy and pleasing to God—this is your true and proper worship. Do not conform to the pattern of this world, but be transformed by the renewing of your mind. Then you will be able to test and approve what God's will is—his good, pleasing and perfect will.

Colossians 3:17
And whatever you do, whether in word or deed, do it all in the name of the Lord Jesus, giving thanks to God the Father through him.

Share with the group:

Just as this section of the curriculum discusses our bodies as the temple of the Holy Spirit with respect to body image and sexual temptation, the same applies to keeping our temples clean. In everything that we do, we should try to glorify God. We will discuss practicing good hygiene in the areas of menstruation, skin care, hair care, and dental care. Don't feel embarrassed to ask any questions. If there is something I'm not

sure of, I will research the answer and get back to you soon.

Distribute the "So Fresh & So Clean" Handout. Review and discuss the information on the handout. Reiterate the need for developing a daily regimen for cleansing their bodies, skin, and teeth; and for taking pride in their appearance and hair care.

Share with the group:

We are about to play a fun game, Personal Hygiene Jeopardy, to help us learn more about how to take care of ourselves in these areas. Don't worry if you don't know all the answers. The purpose is to use the game to learn some tips that we can use to take care of our bodies.

ACTIVITY: Personal Hygiene Jeopardy

To create the Jeopardy game board, use a dry erase board or a piece of flip chart paper. Draw enough lines to create four columns and six rows. Write the four subjects across the top row—Menstruation (Period), Hair Care, Dental Care, Skin Care. Under each subject area, write 100, 200, 300, 400, and 500 in the boxes from the top to the bottom of the column. Repeat for the remaining subject areas. See attached answer sheet for example (do not include the questions or answers on your game board).

Divide the girls into teams. Instruct each team to pick a number from 1-25 to decide the playing order. The team that comes closest to the number you have in mind, without going over it, will start first. The order will follow accordingly.

Read the question that corresponds to the subject area and point value selected by each team. If a team answers a question correctly, add the points to their score. If a team answers a question incorrectly, the other team that raises their hand first will be allowed to answer the question. After all teams have had an opportunity to answer the question, provide the information provided on the answer card. Inform them that there are three "Daily Doubles" included in the game that will allow them to double the point value of the question if they answer it correctly. The team with the most points is the winner. Provide prizes for the winning team.

Depending on the ability of your group, you can choose to adhere to original Jeopardy rules such as losing points when a question is answered incorrectly and making the group provide responses in the form of a question. Otherwise, if you prefer to keep it simple, you can eliminate these rules, let the girls respond however they choose, and only give points when a question is answered correctly. Feel free to adapt this game to fit your group.

DISCUSSION

Based on the activity and the scriptures read, lead the girls in a discussion using the following prompts:

- Did you learn anything new today about taking care of your body? If so, what did you learn?

- Are there any other personal hygiene issues we did not cover today that you still have questions about? (If so, and you are not sure of the answers, tell

the girls you will research their questions and follow up with them at a later date.)

- What's one thing you can do differently to help you think about your body as God's temple?

- In your opinion, what does personal hygiene and taking care of our bodies have to do with our personal relationship with God?

D.I.V.A. CHALLENGE

Share with the group:

This week the D.I.V.A. Challenge is to share one new thing you learned today with another young woman. It can be a friend or family member. Knowledge is power, and once "you know better, you do better."

Tell the girls you will ask them to report on their progress with this challenge at the next session.

CLOSING REFLECTION & PRAYER

Share with the group:

At first glance, it may not seem like our personal hygiene habits have anything to do with our relationship with God. However, in everything we do, we must realize that we serve as representatives of our Heavenly Father. We can give God glory in all things, including taking care of our bodies. This shows Him that we appreciate the gifts and the temple He has given us.

Invite a girl to pray out loud for the group based on the topic discussed. End the session with this prayer:

Father God, thank you for our bodies, your temples. As women, help us realize that taking care of our bodies is another way we give glory to you. Thank you for giving us pride in who we are as your children.

Session 15 Handout:
Tips to Stay So Fresh & So Clean

Menstruation

WHAT'S HAPPENING? A menstrual cycle lasts from the first day of one period to the first day of the next. The typical cycle of an adult female is 28 days, although some are as short as 21 days and others are longer than 35 days. The typical period normally lasts 3-5 days; some are longer and some are shorter. During the cycle, you body releases an egg (ovulation). If the egg is not fertilized by sperm, it will begin to fall apart and shed with the blood lining of your uterus. This causes the bleeding that is known as "your period."

STAYING FRESH & CLEAN It is important to keep your body clean at all times, including when you are having your period. Good hygiene while on your menstrual cycle includes bathing/showering each day to avoid smelling and to feel fresh. Also, change your pad or tampon (sanitary products) every few hours before it is completely full to avoid leaks and smelling. You can select your sanitary products based on how heavy your period is and what activities you are involved in. Try different types of sanitary products to see what feels best. Talk to your mother, older sister, or aunt to help you make a decision. It's a good idea to keep an extra sanitary product in your locker at school in case your period comes unexpectedly. Your menstrual cycle is a physical sign that a girl is capable of becoming pregnant. Although it may be embarrassing at times, having a period is a natural part of life and an example of how we are "fearfully and wonderfully" made by God!

Skin Care

TIPS FOR TEENS

- Wash with lukewarm water and mild soap no more than twice a day. Gently massage in small circles. Don't scrub! It can irritate your skin and make acne worse.
- Use a gentle moisturizer on your face to prevent dryness. Make sure it's oil-free so it doesn't cause blocked pores.
- Drink plenty of water for beautiful skin!
- Avoid a lot of heavy oil and products in your hair because it can seep down into your skin and cause acne.
- Don't squeeze or bust bumps because it can cause scars.
- Wash your hands often, so you don't transfer germs when you touch your face.
- Use sunscreen
- If you wear makeup, wash your face before sleeping to prevent breakouts and clogged pores.
- If you shave, be careful to avoid cutting yourself. Shave lightly, wet your skin, use shave cream, and only shave when you have to.

Source: http://teens.webmd.com/skin-care-teens; www.kidshealth.org

Dental Care

TIPS FOR TEENS

- Brush teeth, gums, and tongue twice a day (morning and night)
- Use fluoride toothpaste
- Floss every day
- Eat healthy foods like fruits and vegetables. Limit candy and other sticky sweets to avoid cavities and puffy/inflamed gums
- Avoid piercings in our mouth areas (tongue, lips, jaw, etc.) to avoid possible infection, nerve damage, bleeding, broken teeth, and damaged tooth enamel Don't smoke! Smoking can stain your teeth and cause puffy/inflamed gums
- See the dentist every 6 months as recommended. Talk to your parents about this.
- Change your toothbrush every 3 months, or sooner if you have been sick

Source: www.youngwomenshealth.org/dental_health.html

Hair Care

TIPS FOR TEENS

- Keep the scalp clean to avoid clogged pores. Scrub your scalp when you wash your hair. Don't oil your scalp more than once a week.
- Wash hair as needed, once every week or two, depending on your life-style. Washing too often can make your hair dry.
- Shampoo and condition in the shower for easier detangling. When detangling hair, always start from the ends and work to the root. Choose a detangling comb based on your hair's thickness. The thicker it is, the wider the teeth should be.
- Use conditioner on the hair, especially the ends, to protect against dryness and damage.
- Avoid frequent use blow-dryers, flat irons, and curling irons. Use a curling iron only when hair is clean.
- Avoid too-tight braids or weaves.
- Trim ends every 6 months.
- Wear a silk scarf or bonnet, or sleep on a satin pillow case at night to avoid breakage

Source: www.essence.com

Session 15 Activity: Personal Hygiene Jeopardy
Questions & Answer Key - Page 1

MENSTRUATION (PERIOD)	HAIR CARE	DENTAL CARE	SKIN CARE
100 True or False - All women get menstrual periods every four weeks. False- Although the general rule is every 28 days, some women's cycles vary from 21 days or longer than 35 (from the start of one period to the start of the next) When you first have your period, it may take a while to regulate. You can track your periods on a calendar to figure out your cycle.	**100** True or False Trimming your ends will keep your hair from growing. False – trimming your ends is one healthy way to prevent breakage and promote hair growth. It's recommended that you clip your ends every 6 months.	**100** What is the name for a hole in the tooth caused by tooth decay? Cavity	**100** True or False- Drinking at least 64 oz. of water per day can keep your skin in healthy condition. True- Staying hydrated (with water) is essential for your body to function properly and dehydration leads to dry skin
200 True or False – You should wash your hands before and after changing your pad or tampon when on your menstrual cycle. True – Hands harbor bacteria (skin is the first line of defense), your vagina is an opening that bacteria could get into.	**200** True or False Using too much hair products can lead to acne. True – Oil build up can clog your pores, travel from your hair to your face and cause acne. Keeping your scalp clean should be part of washing your hair.	**200** How often should you floss your teeth? (DOUBLE) Floss at least once a day every day (end of the day)	**200** True or False - People of color have "built-in" sun protection in their skin. True – People of color have melanin in their skin, which acts like a sun protection. However, it is recommended that they still use sunscreen with SPF 15 (which means you can stay in the sun 15 times longer without burning). The lighter you are, the higher SPF you need.
300 True or False - It is normal to have foul smelling discharge from the vagina False- Although daily discharge is normal for most women, it should not have a bad odor. If you are washing daily, then it could be a sign of infection. Ask your parents to take you to the doctor.	**300** True or False Drinking at least 64 oz. of water per day can help your hair and nails grow, and can make your hair healthier. True- Staying hydrated (with water) is essential for your body to function properly and dehydration leads to brittle nails/hair	**300** Two-part question – How often should you brush your teeth? …and for how long? Brush your teeth at least twice a day (morning and night) for at least 2 minutes each time.	**300** True or False – Scrubbing skin is a good way to remove oil and acne. (DOUBLE) False - scrubbing too often will over-stimulate the oil glands making acne and oil production worse. Harsh scrubbing and popping zits will also leave you with scars from your acne. Wash your face twice a day (no more) with warm water and a mild soap. Gently massage your face with circular motions.

Session 15 Activity: Personal Hygiene Jeopardy
Questions & Answer Key - Page 2

MENSTRUATION (PERIOD)	HAIR CARE	DENTAL CARE	SKIN CARE
400 To maintain proper hygiene, how often should your change your pad or tampon when you are on your period. Every 3-4 hours to prevent staining or odor	**400** True or False – African American hair that is kinky is one of the most sensitive hair types. True- the tighter your coil pattern the more delicate the hair. (Black women are more likely to be balding, detangle in shower with conditioner and wide tooth comb.	**400** How often should you change your toothbrush? Every 3 months, and earlier if you get sick or have a cold	**400** This skin allergy condition, which causes dry, itchy skin, is common among people of color. Eczema – limit length of showers, keep skin moisturized, and avoid extreme temperature fluctuations.
500 True or False - Douching is healthy and should be a regular part of one's hygiene regimen (Double). False- Douching is not recommended by most health care providers. Your vagina naturally cleans itself, and douching can harm the pH balance of your vagina and actually cause infection.	**500** This occasional hair process can keep your hair from excessive dryness and breakage. Deep conditioning treatment –conditioner with plastic cap, under dryer for 10-15 min	**500** Name two activities/behaviors (besides not brushing or flossing) that may have negative effects on your dental health. Eating sugary/sticky foods (cavities), chewing tobacco or smoking (stain teeth and increases risk of oral cancer). Poor nutrition (puffy or inflamed gums), oral piercing (infections, bleeding, and nerve damage in the mouth; damage tooth enamel or break teeth)	**500** Name three key steps to taking care of your skin. Wash, Tone, Moisturize, Exfoliate, Mask (Answers may vary)

Session 16

Hold Out

SESSION GOALS:

D.I.V.A. participants will:
- Understand that abstinence is God's plan for unmarried people
- Learn that God desires us to be sexually pure, which includes our actions AND our thoughts
- Discuss sexual temptation and create a purity plan with strategies to help them resist sexual temptation

SCRIPTURE FOCUS:

1 Corinthians 6:16-20 (Message); 1 Corinthians 10:13 (NLT); Philippians 4:8; 2 Timothy 2:22; Romans 8:1-2; Romans 8:5; James 5:16; Galatians 5:16-21 (NLT); 1 Thessalonians 4:3-8 (NLT); Matthew 5:28

MATERIALS NEEDED:

- D.I.V.A. Handbooks, one book for each girl
- Bibles: Inform the girls to bring Bibles if they have them
- Four children's size jump ropes (available at dollar stores and other inexpensive stores)
- Heavy duty scissors (to cut the rope)
- "Plan Your Purity" Handout
- Pencils or Pens

PREP TASKS:

- Make a copy of the "Plan Your Purity" handout for each girl

----

RECALL (if applicable)

If applicable, follow the directions for facilitating the recall segment described in the introduction on page 18.

CHECK –IN

Make up your own Check-In activity or facilitate the "Highs and Lows" Check-In activity described in the introduction on page 17.

FOUNDATION

Share with the group:

It seems that teens often receive the strongest messages from the church and their parents when it comes to the topic of sex and purity. Through the Bible, God provides specific instructions about when and with whom we should engage in sexual activity. It's not all doom and gloom, though! God designed sex as a beautiful experience to bring a husband and wife closer together and to produce children. Today we will discuss God's purposes for sex, so we can appreciate the beauty of it AND the beauty of holding out until the time is right!

Lead a brief discussion with the group, using the prompts below. Discuss their responses.

- What messages have you received about sex from adults?
- What do you think the Bible says about sex? Why do you think it says that?
- So, what's the big deal about sex if God created it? Why do you think He wants you to abstain from sex before marriage?

Ask someone to read 1 Corinthians 6:16-20 (The Message)

There's more to sex than mere skin on skin. Sex is as much spiritual mystery as physical fact. As written in Scripture, "The two become one." Since we want to become spiritually one with the Master, we must not pursue the kind of sex that avoids commitment and intimacy, leaving us more lonely than ever—the kind of sex that can never "become one." There is a sense in which sexual sins are different from all others. In sexual sin we violate the sacredness of our own bodies, these bodies that were made for God-given and God-modeled love, for "becoming one" with another. Or didn't you realize that your body is a sacred place, the place of the Holy Spirit? Don't you see that you can't live however you please, squandering what God paid such a high price for? The physical part of you is not some piece of property belonging to the spiritual part of you. God owns the whole works. So let people see God in and through your body.

Ask the group for their thoughts on this scripture. Discuss their responses.

Share with the group:

A lot of the messages we get about sex are often to "scare" us into not doing it. We hear, "you will get pregnant" or "you will get a sexually transmitted infection like Herpes or HIV/AIDs." These are real risks that we do not want to play around with, and we can view them as the consequence of being disobedient to God's commands when we have sex outside of marriage. And although we know that having "safe sex" may prevent these consequences, nothing (except abstinence) is 100% safe!

Outside of these physical consequences, there are other spiritual reasons why God wants us to hold out on sexual activity until we are married. Sex is a physical AND spiritual act. It is powerful, and shouldn't be taken lightly! When you have sex with someone, you are giving them a part of yourself both physically and spiritually. This is what the scriptures mean by "two become one." Some people refer to this concept as developing a "soul tie." These soul ties or spiritual connections, if not rooted in God's plan for our lives, can cause a lot of heartache and disruption in our lives. God wants us to hold out for sex—not to punish us—but so we can experience the full joy of sex with our husbands one day.

Use the following illustration to explain the concept of soul ties. Ask for four volunteers, and give each of them a jump rope. Tie the rope around the first volunteer's waist. Loop another rope through the first volunteer's rope one time and then tie it around the second person's waist so they are linked together. Continue this with the other two volunteers until all four are linked to the first volunteer. Ask one of the girls to move forward and draw attention to how the others move with that person. Cut the ropes to show that the ties can be broken, but it is not an easy task.

Share with the group:

In the spiritual realm, this is what happens when we develop ungodly soul ties with others. We carry spiritual and emotional "baggage" from that person forward in our lives. This baggage can affect our future relationship with God and others. Soul ties can be formed through sexual activity or other emotional connections, such as a deep friendship. A soul tie makes it difficult to "get over" a person, and the baggage from one person can move with you through your life.

For example, having an inappropriate sexual relationship as a teenager can linger, and

cause issues with your physical and emotional bond with your husband one day. Soul ties can be broken with prayer and deliverance received from God, but one may have to suffer heavy emotional, physical, and/or spiritual consequences to move past an ungodly soul tie.

Ask the group, "What do you think it means to be sexually pure?" Discuss their responses.

Share with the group:

Sexual purity isn't just about sexual abstinence. Some young people think as long as they are not having sexual intercourse (clarify that this is referencing when a man's penis enters the woman's vagina) that they are sexually pure. They may be participating in activities like heavy petting, making out with their clothes on, watching pornography, or doing more explicit things like having oral sex. However, many think because they haven't had actual intercourse, they are still sexually pure. These activities do not fit within God's definition of sexual purity. Sexual purity includes the things you think, as well as the things you do. Your thoughts lead to actions.

Ask for volunteers to read the following scriptures, and then lead them in a brief discussion on how the scriptures can be connected to this definition of purity.

Philippians 4:8
Finally, brothers and sisters, whatever is true, whatever is noble, whatever is right, whatever is pure, whatever is lovely, whatever is admirable—if anything is

excellent or praiseworthy—think about such things.

Matthew 5:28
But I tell you that anyone who looks at a woman lustfully has already committed adultery with her in his heart.

1 Thessalonians 4:3-8
God's will is for you to be holy, so stay away from all sexual sin. Then each of you will control his own body and live in holiness and honor—not in lustful passion like the pagans who do not know God and his ways. Never harm or cheat a Christian brother in this matter by violating his wife, for the Lord avenges all such sins, as we have solemnly warned you before. God has called us to live holy lives, not impure lives. Therefore, anyone who refuses to live by these rules is not disobeying human teaching but is rejecting God, who gives his Holy Spirit to you.

Galatians 5:16-21 (NLT)
So I say, let the Holy Spirit guide your lives. Then you won't be doing what your sinful nature craves. The sinful nature wants to do evil, which is just the opposite of what the Spirit wants. And the Spirit gives us desires that are the opposite of what the sinful nature desires. These two forces are constantly fighting each other, so you are not free to carry out your good intentions. But when you are directed by the Spirit, you are not under obligation to the law of Moses. When you follow the desires of your sinful nature, the results are very clear: sexual immorality, impurity, lustful pleasures, idolatry, sorcery, hostility, quarreling, jealousy, outbursts of anger, selfish ambition, dissension, division, envy, drunkenness, wild parties, and other sins like these. Let me tell you again, as I have before, that anyone living that sort of life will not inherit the Kingdom of God.

Share with the group:

If you're thinking a lot about sex, and you're fooling around with someone you really like, you're putting yourself in a dangerous place for sexual temptation to overtake you.   This is why God tells us to "think on things that are pure" because once the thought enters our minds we have opened ourselves up to sin.

God designed sex as a way for husband and wife to grow closer, enjoy each other, and produce children. Until then, abstinence is God's plan. If you are having sex outside of this plan God created, you will not get to experience the full benefits of it. You will instead have to deal with consequences—physically, spiritually, and emotionally—for being disobedient to God's commands and rejecting Him. Sexual sin is not just sin committed against God, but a sin you commit against yourself—your own body!

Ask someone to read 2 Timothy 2:22.

Flee the evil desires of youth and pursue righteousness, faith, love and peace, along with those who call on the Lord out of a pure heart.

Share with the group:

Sexual purity is connected to the things you watch, think, say, and hear that may tempt

125

you to engage in sexual relations before marriage. Temptation will always be present. The devil will always attempt to steer you away from God by tempting you with sin. This is especially difficult when it comes to sex because sexual attraction is natural, which means it doesn't go away! This is why the scriptures tell us to flee these desires. Flee literally means to run away! Our own temptations and desires are so powerful, that we will have to flee from them to resist them.

Ask someone to read the following scriptures, and have a brief discussion about how the scriptures can be connected to God's grace and mercy when we mess up in this area.

Romans 8:1-2
Therefore, there is now no condemnation for those who are in Christ Jesus, because through Christ Jesus the law of the Spirit who gives life has set you free from the law of sin and death.

Romans 8:5
Those who live according to the flesh have their minds set on what the flesh desires; but those who live in accordance with the Spirit have their minds set on what the Spirit desires.

James 5:16
Therefore confess your sins to each other and pray for each other so that you may be healed. The prayer of a righteous person is powerful and effective.

1 Corinthians 10:13 (NLT)
The temptations in your life are no different from what others experience. And God is faithful. He will not allow the temptation to be more than you can stand. When you are tempted, he will show you a way out so that you can endure.

Share with the girls

If you have already had sex or failed at your attempts to be abstinent, please know that our God provides second chances and is able to help us refresh our purity! The bible tells us that everyone messes up sometimes, and Jesus' death and resurrection already enables us to overcome every sin that gets us off track. Once we repent, turn away from sin, and make the commitment to get back on track with our sexual purity, God will always provide a way out of tempting situations.

ACTIVITY: PLAN YOUR PURITY

Tell the girls that they will now complete an activity to create a purity plan to brainstorm strategies to resist sexual temptation using four defenses to maintain sexual purity:

1. Having more prayer time and reading the bible for spiritual growth
2. Guarding our eyes and minds from things that don't encourage sexual purity
3. Setting high standards by creating a personal code of conduct
4. Identifying accountability partners

Tell them that not thinking ahead can get them in a lot of trouble. Distribute the "Plan Your Purity" worksheet and the pencils. Instruct them to work on their plans individually, filling in each section on the worksheet.

Once the girls have had some time to complete their worksheets, have them share parts of their plans with the group. Share your thoughts with the group on any commonalities among their plans, strategies suggested to set high standards, and anything else that stands out to you. Ask the girls to share their thoughts on these points as well.

DISCUSSION

Based on the activity and the scriptures read, lead the girls in a discussion using the following prompts:

- What commitments can you make today regarding your interactions with the opposite sex to help you strive for sexual purity?
- What strategies do you think will be helpful to you to "flee" sexual temptation?
- What specific issues present a challenge for you in this area?
- What roles do your friends and family play in helping you to remain sexually pure?
- What support could help you to carry out your purity plan?
- What would you say to other teens to encourage them to live a life of sexual purity?

Ask the group, "Where does dating fit in this discussion? Ask them if they think it's possible to date and maintain their sexual purity? Discuss their responses.

Share with the group:

Some Christians believe that dating is only appropriate if you are considering marrying a person. Others believe that dating is appropriate for young people. Regardless of the view, the main point is to do everything to the glory of God. The Bible does not speak specifically about dating or boyfriend-girlfriend relationships. In reference to romantic relationships, the Bible only speaks of marriage. However, there are many rules for how we should treat each other as brothers and sisters in Christ, and these are what we should pay attention to when dating. If you decide to date, and your parents approve of you doing so, it is very important to maintain high standards in your behavior to remain pure in God's sight. Here are a few suggestions that can help you with resisting sexual temptation when dating (they may have mentioned these already when discussing the worksheet):

- Avoid alone time with boyfriends. If you date, go on group dates instead of one-on-one dates.
- Commit to a high standard for activities you will and will not do. For example, if you set a standard that kissing and rubbing are fine as long as your clothes are on, you are putting yourself at risk for falling victim to temptation. Instead, if you set a standard that you will refrain from this activity altogether, it will help you to remain pure.
- Really use your accountability partners! Be honest talk with them

127

about what's going on, and pray with them for strength in this area.

Before beginning to wrap up the session, share these takeaway points with the group (you can also rephrase them as "true or false" statements to engage the group):

- Some teens think there is no problem with having sex with someone you plan to marry. The main problem here is that sometimes our plans fall through, and until we ARE married, God requires abstinence.

- Kissing can lead to further sexual activity, so this is something to be very mindful of as you try to carry out your purity plan.

- The movies, magazines, web sites, and books you consume can directly affect your sexual purity.

- Remaining abstinent helps you have a clear conscience before God.

- Everyone is NOT having sex. Sometimes teens feel pressured to have sex because they think everyone is doing it. This is not the case. Stand out from the crowd!

- With all our hyper-sexed media, some teens think it is impossible for teenagers to remain pure in the 21st century. Honestly, it is hard, but all things are possible with God!

- If you have already had sex, don't give up or feel defeated. God can restore you and make you sexually pure again.

D.I.V.A. CHALLENGE

Share with the group:
The D.I.V.A. Challenge for this week is to read the reflection scriptures on the "Plan Your Purity" worksheet, and make a commitment to God in your personal prayer time about being sexually pure. Only make the commitment if you are really serious about giving your all to stick with it. Discuss your purity plan with your parents, and enlist an accountability partner to pray with you during this journey. Write about it in your handbook.

Tell the girls you will ask them to report on their progress with this challenge at the next session.

CLOSING REFLECTION & PRAYER

Share with the group:
Sometimes we think that what we do in private is no one else's business, but every part of our lives belong to God and we are responsible for our actions. God calls us to be set apart, and this includes honoring Him with our bodies and being careful to live a sexually pure life. We know that sexual purity does not just include abstaining from sexual intercourse, but it also includes guarding our minds from what we hear, see, and think about it. The Bible tells us that our flesh is weak, so we must flee and resist temptation. Having a plan will help us in our efforts to remain pure and live for Christ!

Invite a girl to pray out loud for the group based on the topic discussed. End the session with this prayer:

Father God, thank you for the beautiful gift of sex you have ordained for husband and wife. We know you are faithful to help us overcome sexual temptation and remain pure in our thoughts and actions. Give us foresight to anticipate tempting situations, send people into our lives that will encourage us as we try to live for you, and help us to understand and demonstrate that our bodies are your temple. Transform our mindset so that we can hold out for your glory.

Session 16 Activity:
Plan Your Purity

No temptation has overtaken you except what is common to mankind. And God is faithful; he will not let you be tempted beyond what you can bear. But when you are tempted, he will also provide a way out so that you can endure it.
1 Corinthians 10:13 (NIV)

Defense #1: Prayer/God's Word

What SPECIFICALLY will you do to strengthen this area?

What sacrifices will you make to grow in this area?

What will you gain from these changes?

Reflection scripture: Galatians 5: 16-17

Defense #2: Guard Your Mind

What music/television/websites will you eliminate to resist sexual temptation?

What will be hard about this?

What will you gain from these changes?

Reflection scripture: Philippians 4:8

Defense #3: Set High Standards

Create four rules for yourself to limit your access to sexually tempting situations. (Ex: I will not be alone with a boy.)

1.

2.

3.

4.

Reflection scripture: 2 Timothy 2:22

Defense #4: Get Accountability!

Write the names of the people who will support your purity. Include parents, friends, trusted adults, etc.

Be care of the company you keep! Write the names of those who may be a bad influence.

Reflection scripture: James 5:16

Session 17

Garbage In, Garbage Out

SESSION GOALS:

D.I.V.A. participants will:

- Understand the concept of "guard your mind" as central to spiritual growth
- Discuss their personal media consumption and its influence on their thoughts, words, and actions
- Learn media literacy concepts to analyze the media messages they receive from various sources

SCRIPTURE FOCUS:

Romans 12:1-2; Philippians 4:8; 1 Corinthians 10:23-24; 1 Corinthians 10:31-33; Ephesians 4:21-24 (NLT)

MATERIALS NEEDED:

- D.I.V.A. Handbooks, one book for each girl
- Bibles: Inform the girls to bring Bibles if they have them
- "Garbage or Not?" Handout
- Song lyrics for four current songs that are popular with the teen demographic
- Radio, Computer, or MP3 player to play the four songs selected
- Flip chart paper (about 10 sheets)
- Markers
- Tape

PREP TASKS:

- Make a copy of the "Garbage or Not?" handout for each girl.

- Print the song lyrics for four current songs. (Prior to the session, ask the girls for suggestions of popular songs teen's listen to; or visit the website of a popular radio station, and select four songs from the songs in current rotation.)

- Download the songs to your MP3 player, burn them to a disc, or locate them on YouTube.com to play them via the Internet. (The first two options may incur a cost to legally download the songs. Listening to the songs via YouTube is usually free.)

- Write the following topics on a piece of flip-chart paper (one per sheet): Favorite song, Favorite movie, Favorite TV show, Favorite song, and Favorite music artist. Hang the sheets up around the room.

RECALL (if applicable)

If applicable, follow the directions for facilitating the recall segment described in the introduction on page 18.

CHECK –IN

Make up your own Check-In activity or facilitate the "Highs and Lows" Check-In activity described in the introduction on page 17.

FOUNDATION

Share with the group:

Today we will be talking about the media we consume, and its effect on our spiritual growth. This includes music, television, movies, websites, and video games. Many people believe that information received from these sources is only for entertainment, and that media does not influence us. However, the Bible is clear that we should be very careful about the information (and the sources of the information) that we have access to, as it can influence our thoughts first, and then our actions and emotions. This is what scripture refers to as "guarding your mind." Media can influence us in positive and negative ways. If we put positive information in our brains, positivity will flow in the way we live our life. If we put garbage into our brains, garbage will come out in our lifestyle. By "garbage," we mean anything that does not align with God's Word and give Him glory. Today we will examine what we are putting in our brains,

and how that information may be influencing us. God wants to be glorified in all parts of our lives, including the media we consume.

ACTIVITY: Top Three

Distribute the markers and instruct the girls to go around the room and write their top three for each topic presented on the flip-chart paper (Favorite song, Favorite movie, Favorite TV show, Favorite song, and Favorite music artist). Tell the girls not to discuss their responses during the activity, but just to write them on each sheet. Tell them you will discuss the responses as a group after everyone has written their top three on each sheet.

Once everyone has written responses on all the sheets, discuss their responses to see if there were any similarities or themes. Ask them to share a little about the subject matter of their top choices and why they like them.

Ask someone to read 1 Corinthians 10:23-24

"I have the right to do anything," you say —but not everything is beneficial. "I have the right to do anything"—but not everything is constructive. No one should seek their own good, but the good of others.

Ask the group, what does this scripture mean? Ask them to think of examples of things they have the "right to do" but that may not be beneficial. Examples include congregating to watch a fight at school or drinking/smoking (over age 21). Ask them, "How does this verse help you as you think about some of the top choices you wrote down?"

Share with the group:

Although there are many actions that are lawful or within our rights to do, it does not mean that those actions are helpful to our spiritual growth. Of course, listening to a sexy song is not going to send you to hell. However, if that song fills your mind with sexual thoughts that may tempt you to sin, it's not worth it to continue listening to it. Although it may not be "wrong" to listen to it, you should be asking yourself, "Does listening to this help me to be more like God?" God wants us to be more like Him— in every thought, word, and action. Just because we CAN do something, doesn't mean we SHOULD do it. Also, the last part of 1 Corinthians 10:24 says, "No one should seek their own good, but the good of others." We have a commitment to not ruin our Christian witness to others we may encounter. If someone who doesn't know God is turned off from Him because they see you doing, watching, or listening to something that seems like it doesn't match your faith, that is a problem. Even if you can continue doing that without feeling guilty, you should stop so that it won't keep that person from learning more about your faith and your God.

Ask someone to read 1 Corinthians 10:31-33

So whether you eat or drink or whatever you do, do it all for the glory of God. Do not cause anyone to stumble, whether Jews, Greeks or the church of God— even as I try to please everyone in every way. For I am not seeking my own good but the good of many, so that they may be saved.

Ask the group, "What connections can you make between this scripture and our discussion so far?"

Share with the group:

Popular music and TV often hypes up reckless sexual behavior, violence, and seeking temporary thrills without thinking about the consequences. These themes are not in keeping with the Bible's instructions to "do it all to the glory of God." If we believe that our thoughts are influenced by what we see and hear, the best thing may be to cut out destructive media influences completely. However, this is not always realistic since we are bombarded with media everywhere we go, and we may not always have control over what is being played. Everything on the TV, radio, and web isn't bad, so how do we filter out the garbage from the good stuff and guard our minds so we are not negatively influenced? (Discuss their responses to this question.)

Ask someone to read the following scriptures:

Romans 12:1-2
Therefore, I urge you, brothers and sisters, in view of God's mercy, to offer your bodies as a living sacrifice, holy and pleasing to God—this is your true and proper worship. Do not conform to the pattern of this world, but be transformed by the renewing of your mind. Then you will be able to test and approve what God's will is—his good, pleasing and perfect will.

Philippians 4:8
Finally, brothers and sisters, whatever is true, whatever is noble, whatever is right, whatever is pure, whatever is lovely, whatever is admirable—if anything is excellent or praiseworthy—think about such things.

Ephesians 4:21-24 (NLT)
Since you have heard about Jesus and have learned the truth that comes from him, throw off your old sinful nature and your former way of life, which is corrupted by lust and deception. Instead, let the Spirit renew your thoughts and attitudes. Put on your new nature, created to be like God—truly righteous and holy.

Ask the group, how do these scriptures help us to make decisions about what we continue to watch/hear and what we need to eliminate from our lives? Discuss their responses.

Share with the group:

Notice that the common factor from these last three scriptures is that they all deal with the mind. We are transformed by having a renewed mind, which means that through reading God's word, our perspective about life, and ourselves, changes. We are instructed to think on things that are pure and praiseworthy. All of this emphasis is on our minds because our thoughts are very powerful.

Ask the girls to think of a time when their thoughts were so strong towards something that it ended up dictating their behavior.

Examples may include thinking so much about making out with her boyfriend, that she got carried away the next time she saw him. Or, having feelings of jealousy towards another girl that lead to a fight. Discuss their responses.

Share with the group:

Thoughts lead to actions! Those actions can either be sinful and pull us away from God, or be righteous and pull us towards Him. Remember, it all starts in the mind so guard your mind! Here are a few simple questions to help you when you are listening to music, watching television, surfing the Internet. Ask yourself:

- Am I getting something from this to help me be more like God?
- Is God getting any glory out of this?
- If Jesus were standing over my shoulder watching/listening to this with me, would He like this? Would He be okay with me seeing or hearing this?

Answering these questions honestly will help you analyze media and start to make some decisions about the media you consume. We are going to practice now with a few popular songs that are out now.

ACTIVITY: Garbage or Not?

Divide the girls into four groups. Distribute a song, a copy of the "Garbage or Not?" handout, markers, and a piece of flip chart paper to each group. Tell them to review the song lyrics and analyze the songs using the questions on the handout. Tell them to use the flipchart paper to record their responses, and to designate a speaker form the group to present their ideas back to the large group.

After each group finishes answering the questions, play a clip of each song. Give the groups a few more minutes to add any additional comments to their sheets after hearing the songs played. Ask each group speaker to report the groups' findings back to the large group.

DISCUSSION

Based on the activity and the scriptures read, lead the girls in a discussion using the following prompts:

- What are your thoughts of these songs based on the scriptures we read today? Are they garbage or not? Do they bring glory to God?

- If Jesus were standing over your shoulder, do you think He would like the music? Why or why not?

- What are some themes that the songs have in common? Do you think these themes align with God's word?

- Are any of the songs we discussed today songs you have heard, but never paid attention to the lyrics? If so, what are your thoughts now that you have studied the lyrics? Did anything surprise you?

- Was there any difference in the song's impact for you just reading the lyrics versus actually hearing the song played? If so, what do you think accounts for the difference?

- Does this session cause you to want to make any changes about any of the media you consume, including TV, movies, songs, video games, and websites?

D.I.V.A. CHALLENGE

Share with the group:
The D.I.V.A. Challenge for this week is to read Philippians 4:8, and select at least one ungodly media source that does not glorify God from your life to eliminate. It may be music by a particular artist, a certain T.V. show, or a website you visit often. Pray about your decision and think about your reasons for choosing this particular source. Ask yourself these questions to make your decision:

- Am I getting something from this to help me be more like God?
- Is God getting any glory out of this?
- If Jesus were standing over my shoulder watching/listening to this with me, would He like this? Would He be okay with me seeing or hearing this?

Write about it in your handbook.

Tell the girls you will ask them to report on their progress with this challenge at the next session.

135

CLOSING REFLECTION & PRAYER

Share with the group:

Remember God wants to be glorified in every part of our lives. We must take a good look at anything that causes us to stumble or causes someone else to stumble on our journey to be more like Him. The media that influence our thoughts and actions are included.

Invite a girl to pray out loud for the group based on the topic discussed. End the session with this prayer:

Father God, thank you for bringing this knowledge to our attention. Give us the strength to gravitate towards things in our lives that lead us to be more like you. Allow us to really examine the things in our lives to see if they bring you glory. We realize that only the things we do for you will last. Help us to grow in this area. We thank you in advance for the growth and renewed mind that you offer.

Session 17 Activity:
Garbage or Not?

Work with your group to analyze the lyrics of your assigned song
using the questions below.

* **What do you like about this song?**

* **What do you dislike about this song?**

* **What is the purpose or main message of this song? Who is it intended for?**

* **What values or themes are present in this song?**

* **What values or themes are missing from this song?**

* **What ways do you think people will be affected by this music?**

* **How might other people understand the message of this song differently?**

*Some of these questions were adapted from the Center for Media Literacy - www.medialit.org.

DEALING WITH OTHERS
Sessions 18-22

Theme Overview:

This theme focuses on strengthening our relationships with others and helping us learn God's design for our interactions with others. Whether it's romantic relationships, parental relationships, or friendships—God desires that our interactions with others are a reflection of Him and His love. Additionally, this theme will cover topics such as improving our communication skills, sharing our faith with others, and community service. When Jesus was asked what the greatest commandment was, He stated that the first was to love God with everything we have and the second was to love others as we love ourselves. This scripture is central for all the sessions, and can be found in Mark 12:29-31:

"The most important one," answered Jesus, "is this: 'Hear, O Israel: The Lord our God, the Lord is one. Love the Lord your God with all your heart and with all your soul and with all your mind and with all your strength.' The second is this: 'Love your neighbor as yourself.' There is no commandment greater than these."

Through these sessions, girls are encouraged to think of how they treat others as a representation of their love for God. Through these lessons, the girls will learn that receiving God's love also requires that we give it to others, and that love is evident in the way we treat others.

Session 18
What About Your Friends?

SESSION GOALS:

D.I.V.A. participants will:
- Use scripture to analyze and reflect on their own friendships
- Review scripture that instructs on how to treat others
- Reflect on changes they may need to make in their friendships

SCRIPTURE FOCUS:

2 Corinthians 6:14 (NLT); 1 Corinthians 13:4-8; Luke 6:31; Matthew 6:14-16; Proverbs 18:24; Proverbs 27:17 (NLT); John 15:12-17 (NLT)

MATERIALS NEEDED:

- D.I.V.A. Handbooks, one book for each girl
- Bibles: Inform the girls to bring Bibles if they have them
- Flip chart paper (10-11 sheets)
- Markers

PREP TASKS:

- Write the prompts from the "Friendship Reflection" activity on flip chart paper and post them around the room (one prompt per sheet)

RECALL (if applicable)

If applicable, follow the directions for facilitating the recall segment described in the introduction on page 18.

CHECK –IN

Make up your own Check-In activity or facilitate the "Highs and Lows" Check-In activity described in the introduction on page 17.

FOUNDATION

Share with the group:

Many of us have heard the term; "Birds of a feather flock together." This saying simply means that we are very similar (or we eventually become similar) to the people we hang around. The people we call "friends" says a lot about us. During the teenage years, our friends have a lot of influence over us. Your friends can encourage you to follow Christ, or they can steer you away from God's purpose for your life. You have the same influence on them. This is why it is so important to choose your friends wisely.

Today we will discuss our friendships, and explore both our role as friends to others and the friends that are currently in our lives.

Lead a brief discussion with the group, using the prompts below. Discuss their responses.

- Would you say your friendships are healthy or unhealthy relationships? Why or why not?
- Many girls believe that girls cannot be friends without arguing, jealousy, and drama. Do you agree or disagree? Why or Why Not?

ACTIVITY: FRIENDSHIP REFLECTION

Distribute markers to the girls and instruct them to go around the room and write their responses on each of the flip chart sheets to complete the sentence.

- Use these prompts for the flip chart sheets:
  - My friends treat me like….
  - My friends treat other people like…
  - My friendships make my life better because…
  - My friendships make my life worse because…
  - My friends respect themselves in the following ways…
  - My friends disrespect themselves in the following ways…
  - I am a good friend because…
  - My choice of friends says that I am…
  - Qualities of a good friend include….

After everyone has had an opportunity to write their comments on the sheets, review and discuss their responses. Ask for specific examples of their responses based on their current friendships.

Ask the girls, "What instructions do you think God gives us in the Bible about how we should choose our friends?" Discuss their responses.

Ask for volunteers to read the following scriptures:

2 Corinthians 6:14 (NLT)
Don't team up with those who are unbelievers. How can righteousness be a partner with wickedness? How can light live with darkness?

Proverbs 27:17 (NLT)
As iron sharpens iron, so a friend sharpens a friend.

Share with the group:

To be "yoked" means to be joined or linked to another person. Scripture cautions us from forming close relationships with unbelievers, so that we will not be tempted to engage in activity that will draw us away from God and His plan for our lives. This doesn't mean that we can't talk to unbelievers. Jesus spent time with unbelievers so that they could become to know Him and eventually believe. In the same way, our interaction with unbelievers is to show them God in us, and to lead them to salvation. However, our close friends should be individuals that know God, too, and can encourage us in our Christian walk. Our friends ARE major influencers in our decision-making. Remember "birds of a feather flock together." God desires that we seek out close friends that are also seeking Him, so that when we are struggling or need encouragement in our Christian walk, they can help us to get back on track. This is what the scripture means by "iron sharpens iron."

Divide the group into four smaller groups. Give each of the groups one of the scriptures below. Tell them to read the scripture and discuss how the scripture applies to friendships using the following discussion prompts (You may want to write them on the board or a sheet of paper):

- After reading this scripture, what conclusions can you make about how you should choose your friends?
- After reading this scripture, what conclusions can you make about how friends should treat each other?
- If you hold your current friendships up to these scriptures, what are your thoughts about them?

After the groups have had time to discuss, bring them back together as a large group and have each group share their thoughts about their assigned scripture and its connection to friendship.

1 Corinthians 13:4-8
Love is patient, love is kind. It does not envy, it does not boast, it is not proud. It does not dishonor others, it is not self-seeking, it is not easily angered, it keeps no record of wrongs. Love does not delight in evil but rejoices with the truth. It always protects, always trusts, always hopes, always perseveres. Love never fails. But where there are prophecies, they will cease; where there are tongues, they will

be stilled; where there is knowledge, it will pass away.

Luke 6:31
Do to others as you would have them do to you.

Matthew 6:14-16
For if you forgive other people when they sin against you, your heavenly Father will also forgive you. But if you do not forgive others their sins, your Father will not forgive your sins.

Proverbs 18:24
One who has unreliable friends soon comes to ruin, but there is a friend who sticks closer than a brother.

Return to the piece of paper on the flip chart with the prompt "Qualities of a good friend include…" from the "Friendship Reflection" activity above. Ask the girls, based on the discussion so far, if there are any new qualities we need to add to this sheet." Add characteristics such as trust, honesty, dependability, communication, love, and respect to this list if the girls have not mentioned these traits. Tell the girls that these are all characteristics of a healthy relationship.

Ask the girls, "If these are characteristics of a healthy relationship, what are the characteristics of an unhealthy relationship?" Brainstorm a list with them and write it on a new piece of paper. If they are stuck, tell them to think of the opposite of the words on the sheet. Add characteristics such as control, jealousy, dishonesty, intimidation, humiliation, and disrespect to the list if the girls have not mentioned these traits.

Share with the group:

The healthy relationship traits are the characteristics of true friends. A person that puts you down with negative words, bullies you, uses negative peer pressure to intimidate you to exhibit negative behaviors, constantly wants to fight with you, seeks to embarrass and humiliate you, or abuses you in ANY way, is not your friend. As God's children, we are an extension of Him, and should not be mistreated by anyone. Likewise, we should not mistreat others.

Ask for someone to read John 15:12-17 (NLT)

This is my commandment: Love each other in the same way I have loved you. There is no greater love than to lay down one's life for one's friends. You are my friends if you do what I command. I no longer call you slaves, because a master doesn't confide in his slaves. Now you are my friends, since I have told you everything the Father told me. You didn't choose me. I chose you. I appointed you to go and produce lasting fruit, so that the Father will give you whatever you ask for, using my name. This is my command: Love each other.

Share with the group:

In this passage of scripture, Jesus commands us to love each other and treat others how we want to be treated. This applies to all our relationships. Jesus also shows us that He is the ultimate example of a good friend because He gave His life for us. He explains that He has called us friends, and has shared all of His knowledge with us through the Bible. Wow, do you believe that? Jesus, our Lord and Savior, chose us as His friends! And He commands that we show that we know

Him by showing the love He gave to us to our friends. All of the scriptures we've read today show us clearly that being a friend carries a heavy responsibility. It is not just about partying and hanging out together. Being a true friend requires that we love our friends, forgive them, and hold them accountable to live for God.

DISCUSSION

Based on the activity and the scriptures read, lead the girls in a discussion using the following prompts:

- Based on the scriptures we've read today, what grade would you give yourself as a friend? How would you grade your close friends?
- The Bible does not speak about boyfriend/girlfriend relationships. With regard to romantic relationships, it only speaks about marriage. How do you think the scriptures we've read today apply to boyfriend/girlfriend relationships?
- What are some areas you could improve in as a friend? What specifically will you do to be a better friend?
- How can we apply these scriptures to peer pressure?
- Are there any current friendships that you need to change or end based on information we discussed today?
- Is anyone dealing with negative peer pressure from friends? How will you deal with this according to the scriptures we discussed today?
- Is anyone being bullied or bullying someone else? How will you deal with this according to the scriptures we discussed today?

D.I.V.A. CHALLENGE

Share with the group:

The D.I.V.A. Challenge for this week is to reread the scriptures in this session, pray and reflect on your current friendships. If you are holding a grudge, talk with the person face to face to deal with the issue with love and forgiveness. If you have not been a good friend, talk with the person face to face and ask for forgiveness. If you have a friend that has not been a good friend to you, talk with the person face to face to deal with the issue with love. Pray before you act, and talk about these issues with an adult you trust.

Write about it in your handbook.

Tell the girls you will ask them to report on their progress with this challenge in the next session.

CLOSING REFLECTION & PRAYER

Share with the group:

Friends play a very important role in our lives. Through our friendships, we have an opportunity to show God's love to others. We also have the opportunity to receive God's love. Just as with everything else in our lives, God wants to get the glory out of our friendships. Our position as a child of God should be honored both in how we treat and how our friends treat us.

Invite a girl to pray out loud for the group based on the topic discussed. End the session with this prayer:

Father, we love you. Thank you for saving us and choosing us as your friends. We are honored and humbled that you would call us "friend." Help us to show your love to others so that we may be living examples of the friendship you give to us. Forgive us for not always treating others as we want to be treated. Bring our actions to our attention so we may repent and strive daily to be more like you. Help us to realize our worth as your children, so that we may choose friends that draw us closer to you. Be glorified in our friendships.

Session 19

Honor & Obey

SESSION GOALS:

D.I.V.A. participants will:
- Review and discuss the responsibilities of parents and children according to scripture
- Discuss the parallels between their spiritual father and their earthly parents and caregivers
- Express their feelings to their parents through a written letter

SCRIPTURE FOCUS:

Proverbs 3:11-12; 1 Timothy 5:8; Colossians 3:20-21; Proverbs 12:1; Proverbs 22:6; Ephesians 6:1-4 (NLT); Colossians 3:20; Proverbs 13:24 (NLT); Psalm 68:5; Psalm 27:9-10 (MSG)

MATERIALS NEEDED:

- D.I.V.A. Handbooks, one book for each girl
- Bibles: Inform the girls to bring Bibles if they have them
- Flip chart paper
- Markers
- Tape
- "Letter to My Parents" Activity Handout
- Extra sheets of blank paper for the "Letter to My Parents" Activity
- Pens (one for each girl)

PREP TASKS:

- Make copies of the "Letter to My Parents" activity handout (one per girl)
- Label one sheet of flip chart "Parents Responsibilities" and another sheet "Children's Responsibilities" and post them on the wall

----

RECALL (if applicable)

If applicable, follow the directions for facilitating the recall segment described in the introduction on page 18.

CHECK –IN

Make up your own Check-In activity or facilitate the "Highs and Lows" Check-In activity described in the introduction on page 17.

FOUNDATION

Share with the group:

For some teens, their relationship with their parents can be very frustrating at times. Since we don't choose our parents, this is one area of our lives where we have little control. At times, you could be getting along great, and at other times, you feel as if you can't wait to grow up and get out of their house. Sometimes our parents are not around to raise us, and other family members or adults step in to parent us. Sometimes parents may be separated or divorced, and this can be a very stressful environment for their children. Despite whether you feel like you have the best or worst parents, the Bible gives us instructions regarding our relationship with our parents. Today we will learn more about God's Word as it relates to interacting with our parents and caregivers, and how we can honor God by honoring our parents.

Ask the group, "If you had to choose one word to describe your relationship with your parents, what would it be?" Discuss their responses.

Draw the girls' attention to the flip chart sheets posted in the room. Explain that the group will read scriptures and discuss the responsibilities of parents and children indicated in each scripture. Explain that the sheet labeled "Parents Responsibilities" will be used to list responsibilities parents have to their children, and the sheet labeled "Children's Responsibilities" will be used to list responsibilities children have to their parents.

Assign volunteers to read the following scriptures. Stop and discuss each scripture after it is read, and have the girls brainstorm responsibilities indicated in the scriptures. Assign a writer for each sheet to put their responses on the appropriate sheet.

Proverbs 3:11-12
My son, do not despise the Lord's discipline, and do not resent his rebuke, because the Lord disciplines those he loves, as a father the son he delights in.

1 Timothy 5:8
Anyone who does not provide for their relatives, and especially for their own household, has denied the faith and is worse than an unbeliever.

Colossians 3:20-21
Children, obey your parents in everything, for this pleases the Lord. Fathers, do not embitter your children, or they will become discouraged.

Proverbs 12:1
Whoever loves discipline loves knowledge, but whoever hates correction is stupid.

Proverbs 22:6
Start children off on the way they should go, and even when they are old they will not turn from it.

Ephesians 6:1-4 (NLT)
Children, obey your parents because you belong to the Lord, for this is the right thing to do. "Honor your father and mother." This is the first commandment with a promise: If you honor your father and mother, "things will go well for you, and you will have a long life on the

earth." **Fathers, do not provoke your children to anger by the way you treat them. Rather, bring them up with the discipline and instruction that comes from the Lord.**

Colossians 3:20
Children, obey your parents in everything, for this pleases the Lord.

Proverbs 13:24 (NLT)
Those who spare the rod of discipline hate their children. Those who love their children care enough to discipline them.

Review their responses, add your responses, and add the following roles to the list if they are not mentioned in the conversation.

Responsibilities of Parents:
- Lead their children to develop a personal relationship with God
- Provide love
- Model God's love by their words and actions
- Provide guidance
- Educate on life skills (respect, communication skills, etc.)
- Provide discipline
- Provide basic needs (food, shelter, clothes, etc.)
- Provide protection and safety
- Encourage and support

Responsibilities of Children:
- Show love in your words and actions
- Obey
- Respect and honor them
- Readily accept and seek out guidance from parents

Ask the group, "What specific behaviors do your parents demonstrate to carryout these responsibilities?" Discuss their responses.

Ask the group, "What does it look like to respect and honor your parents? What specific behaviors can you demonstrate to show your parents that you obey and respect them?" Discuss their responses. Suggest examples such as eliminating back talk or disrespectful language, following their rules, sharing concerns in a respectful manner, helping with chores around the house, etc. if the girls don't mention them.

Share with the group:

From the scriptures we've covered, we see that parents are intended to be a blessing to us, and we are intended to be a blessing to them. By carrying out our biblical responsibilities, we earn trust and most importantly, honor God. You may clash with your parents at time because their job is to prepare you for adulthood, and this means that at times they will have to correct and discipline you to guide you in the right direction. Our parents are not perfect, but their job is to serve as an earthly example of what our Heavenly Father is to us.

Ask the girls, "Is anyone being raised by someone other than their biological parents?" If they are comfortable discussing, ask them to share their feelings about this, and their thoughts about their biological parents.

Ask someone to read Psalm 68:5

A father to the fatherless, a defender of widows, is God in his holy dwelling.

Ask someone to read Psalm 27:9-10 (MSG)

You've always been right there for me; don't turn your back on me now. Don't throw me out, don't abandon me; you've always kept the door open. My father and mother walked out and left me, but God took me in.

Share with the group:

Some of our parents have challenges. Some are absent, and have not been there all the time or at all. Parents will eventually have to deal with the consequences of their actions; and, unfortunately, sometimes their innocent children have to deal with the consequences of their actions too. The light in this tough situation is that our Heavenly Father is a "father to the fatherless." Through Him all of us can experience the love of a father, and even though it is very difficult, He gives us the strength to forgive our parents. He will never leave us.

ACTIVITY: LETTER TO MY PARENTS

Distribute the "Letter to My Parents" worksheet, and give the girls some quiet time to write a letter to their parents. Encourage them to pray before writing, and share what's on their hearts in the letter. Have extra paper on hand in case they need additional sheets. After the girls have had some time to write, invite them to share their letter with the group if they feel comfortable. Provide any words of wisdom you can share based on the content of the letters. Tell them sharing their letters with their parents may be a good way to talk with their parents about their relationship.

DISCUSSION

Based on the activity and the scriptures read, lead the girls in a discussion using the following prompts:

- What about your parents makes you grateful? How can you show your appreciation?
- In what ways does God bless you through your parents?
- In what area is your relationship with your parents really strong? What area is it weak?
- How do you think you can strengthen your relationship with your parents?
- In what ways do you think you can honor God's word to obey and respect your parents if they are engaging in negative behaviors, or if they have not always been there for you?
- You can be a blessing to your parents by praying for them. In what areas do you think you should pray for your parents?
- Based on the scriptures we've read today, are there particular areas you think you need to work on as far as respecting your parents?
- Based on our discussion today, are there specific areas you would like to discuss with your parents to strengthen your relationship?

D.I.V.A. CHALLENGE

Share with the group:

The D.I.V.A. Challenge for this week is to share your letter or part of the letter you wrote in the session with your parents. The purpose of this is to try and build understanding between you and your parent through a conversation about your true feelings. Be respectful when sharing your letter, and pray about it before you share it. Use this as an opportunity to learn more about your parents, and for them to learn more about you. If you feel uncomfortable discussing your letter out loud with your parents or caregivers, ask them to read your letter silently, and to write a letter back to you. If you don't feel safe or comfortable talking to your parents, hold your letter and pray about a good time to talk with your parents. You may want to discuss your feelings about this with a trusted adult like a spiritual leader, mentor, or family member.

Write about it in your handbook.

Tell the girls you will ask them to report on their progress with this challenge at the next session.

CLOSING REFLECTION & PRAYER

Share with the group:

Our parents are not perfect, and they will make mistakes. Despite this, God commands that we respect our parents. Most parents are doing the best they can based on the knowledge they have. We must pray for our parents. If your parent is not acting in a way that makes you feel safe, share your concerns with another family member or adult you trust to get assistance on how to handle the issue.

Invite a girl to pray out loud for the group based on the topic discussed. End the session with this prayer:

Father, we come to you with gratitude in our hearts, knowing we will always have a loving parent in you. Forgive us for times when we have been disrespectful or disobedient to our parents. Help us to honor them in our words and actions both when we are with them and when we are away. We pray that they seek you for wisdom in how to parent us. We pray that they find salvation in you, and they experience your love so that they may give it back to us. If our parents have hurt us, or if we have broken relationships with them, we pray for healing and restoration to make our relationships with our parents whole. Help us to forgive, so that we may receive your forgiveness. Help our parents to see and appreciate us as a gift from you.

Take a few minutes to be quiet and pray to the Lord before you start writing. Share your love and share your hurt. Ask the Lord to help you to remain respectful and write a letter to your parents to share what's on your heart. Use additional paper if needed.

Dear _____,

_____

_____

_____

_____

_____

_____

_____

_____

_____

_____

_____

_____

Session 20

Say What!?!?!

SESSION GOALS:

D.I.V.A. participants will:

- Learn instructions from scripture about the type of communication glorifies God
- Review communication tips that help build understanding with others
- Practice using healthy communication tips through role-play scenarios

SCRIPTURE FOCUS:

Proverbs 18:21 (Message); Luke 6:45 (NLT); James 3:6-10; Proverbs 18:8 (Message); Ephesians 5:3-4 (Message); 2 Timothy 2:22-26 (Message); Ephesians 4:29-32 (Message); Psalm 19:14

MATERIALS NEEDED:

- D.I.V.A. Handbooks, one book for each girl
- Bibles: Inform the girls to bring Bibles if they have them
- Flip Chart Paper
- Markers
- Pens (One for each girl)
- Say What?!?! Communication Tips Handout
- Say What?!?! Role-Play Scenarios Activity sheet

PREP TASKS:

- Copy the Say What?!?! Communication Tips Handout (one per girl)
- Copy the Say What?!?! Role-Play Scenarios Activity sheet (one copy for each group of 3-4 girls)

RECALL (if applicable)

If applicable, follow the directions for facilitating the recall segment described in the introduction on page 18.

CHECK –IN

Make up your own Check-In activity or facilitate the "Highs and Lows" Check-In activity described in the introduction on page 17.

FOUNDATION

Share with the group:

We all have heard that old saying, "Sticks and stones may break my bones but words will never hurt me," and we also know that the saying isn't true. Some of the most painful experiences often are when someone you love or care for says some really hurtful words to you. Scripture provides many instructions on how we should use our words. It tells us that our words are powerful! The Bible also tells us that if we learn to control the words that come out of our mouths, we will experience positive benefits in our lives. Today we will talk about communication; and how to use our words to build understanding with others and to glorify God.

Ask the group, "What is communication? What are the different types of communication?" Discuss their responses.

Share with the group:

Communication is the sharing of thoughts between two or more people. Communication involves a speaker and listener, which are sometimes referred to as the messenger and receiver. Verbal communication is sharing messages through our spoken words and voice tone. Non-verbal communication is sharing messages through our body language, facial expressions, and eye contact. Communication can also be in the written form.

Ask for volunteers to read the following scriptures. Discuss the girls' thoughts on the meaning of each scripture and provide the comments below each scripture during the discussion.

Proverbs 18:21 (MSG)
Words kill, words give life; they're either poison or fruit—you choose.

This is a powerful scripture. Our words can build up a person or tear them down, and we control this.

Ask the girls to
- Share about a time they used words to "give life" to a situation or person.
- Share about a time when they used words to hurt a situation or a person.
- Share about a time when another's words either built them up or tore them down.

For each situation shared, ask them to also share the outcome of the situation.

Luke 6:45 (NLT)
A good person produces good things from the treasury of a good heart, and an evil person produces evil things from the treasury of an evil heart. What you say flows from what is in your heart.

Ask the girls, "Have you ever experienced someone saying something hurtful, and then saying 'they didn't mean it like that' after it was clear that your feelings were hurt? How did that make you feel? Did you believe them?" Discuss their responses.

The words we use to express ourselves are indications about how we really feel about others, ourselves, and the world around us. Letting God work on our hearts and minds to transform us from the inside out through His Word and a relationship with Him, will help us strengthen our communication with others.

James 3:6-10
The tongue also is a fire, a world of evil among the parts of the body. It corrupts the whole body, sets the whole course of one's life on fire, and is itself set on fire

151

by hell. All kinds of animals, birds, reptiles and sea creatures are being tamed and have been tamed by mankind, but no human being can tame the tongue. It is a restless evil, full of deadly poison. With the tongue we praise our Lord and Father, and with it we curse human beings, who have been made in God's likeness. Out of the same mouth come praise and cursing. My brothers and sisters, this should not be.

Ask the girls, "What are your thoughts on this scripture? Do you have a hard time controlling your tongue? Why do you think it's so hard to control it?"

This scripture teaches us that what comes out of our mouth today can affect us for the rest of our lives! Wow! This tells us that we have to choose our words carefully. The Bible discusses several types of conversation we should stay away from, and the consequences of engaging in them.

Ask for volunteers to read the following scriptures. As the group reads and discusses each scripture, tell the girls to identify types of conversation we should avoid according to the scripture. Write their responses on a piece of flip chart paper. Share the comments provided.

Proverbs 18:8 (MSG)
Listening to gossip is like eating cheap candy; do you really want junk like that in your belly?

Ephesians 5:3-4 (MSG)
Don't allow love to turn into lust, setting off a downhill slide into sexual promiscuity, filthy practices, or bullying greed. Though some tongues just love the taste of gossip, those who follow Jesus have better uses for language than that. Don't talk dirty or silly. That kind of talk doesn't fit our style. Thanksgiving is our dialect.

2 Timothy 2:22-26 (MSG)
Run away from infantile indulgence. Run after mature righteousness—faith, love, peace—joining those who are in honest and serious prayer before God. Refuse to get involved in inane discussions; they always end up in fights. God's servant must not be argumentative, but a gentle listener and a teacher who keeps cool, working firmly but patiently with those who refuse to obey. You never know how or when God might sober them up with a change of heart and a turning to the truth, enabling them to escape the Devil's trap, where they are caught and held captive, forced to run his errands.

This scripture encourages us to be mature, and avoid "empty" or "useless" conversation. In addition to causing unnecessary conflict, engaging in this negative conversation can also ruin your Christian witness. This means that because of your negative behavior, you can turn someone off from learning more about the God you say that you serve.

Ephesians 4:29-32 (MSG)
Watch the way you talk. Let nothing foul or dirty come out of your mouth. Say only what helps, each word a gift. Don't grieve God. Don't break his heart. His Holy Spirit, moving and breathing in you, is the most intimate part of your life, making you fit for himself. Don't take such a gift for granted. Make a clean break with all cutting, backbiting, profane

talk. *Be gentle with one another, sensitive. Forgive one another as quickly and thoroughly as God in Christ forgave you.*

Ask the girls, "What are your reactions to this scriptures reference of 'breaking God's heart' by using foul language to tear others down?" Discuss their responses

Review the responses on the flip chart paper. Ask the girls if they have any more "conversations to avoid" based on the scriptures just read. Add any responses you have come up with, and add the following roles to the list if they are not mentioned in the conversation.

Conversations to Avoid:
- Gossip
- Profanity and other foul language
- Crass jokes and language (i.e. inappropriately sexual, racist, etc.)
- Useless arguing
- Talking about others behind their back (backbiting)
- Harsh and critical words directed towards others (cutting talk)

Ask the group, "Which of these types of conversation have you received from others. How did that make you feel?" Discuss their responses.

Ask the group, "Which of these types of conversation have you used towards others?" How do you think that made them feel?" Discuss their responses.

Ask someone to read, Psalm 19:14

May these words of my mouth and this meditation of my heart be pleasing in your sight, Lord, my Rock and my Redeemer.

Share with the group:

This scripture should be our prayer to God as we communicate to others, especially when we are upset. A lot of times we find ourselves using negative language because we are angry, upset, jealous, etc. Sometimes we are trying to get back at another person whose words or actions hurt us, so we want to try and hurt them back. Even when we are upset, we still want our words to be pleasing in His sight. If we don't practice self-control in our communication, we can find ourselves disappointing God and being out of fellowship with others in our life. We can express our anger, irritation, or disappointment with others without being hurtful or rude. How you say something is often just as important as what you say. When we use good communication skills, genuine understanding can take place and conflict is more likely to be resolved.

Distribute the "Say What?!?! Communication Tips" Handout. Ask the girls for real life scenarios to practice using the "I Message" strategy with them. Review and discuss the information on the handout. Do your best to answer any questions the girls may have.

ACTIVITY: SAY WHAT?!?! ROLE PLAY

Divide the girls into groups. Distribute the "Say What?!?! Role-Play Scenarios" Activity sheet. Assign a scenario to each group. Tell the girls to read the scenario as a group, discuss it, and determine a scripture at the bottom of the page that would be useful for the character in the scenario to read. The girls can also use their own real-life scenarios for this activity as well. Then, each group should develop a brief 1-2 minute role-play to illustrate a way to use some of the communication tips on the handout that was just reviewed. Allow the groups about 10-15 minutes to discuss and prepare their 1-2 minute role-play. Each group then should present their role-play to the larger group.

DISCUSSION

Discuss the scenarios, scriptures, and communication tips the groups displayed in their role-plays. Based on the activity and the scriptures read, lead the girls in a discussion using the following prompts:

- Why do you think it is so hard for us to choose to use the healthier communication you displayed in your role-plays?
- Communication is a learned skilled that is influenced by your upbringing, family, environment, and life experiences. In what ways has your family influenced your communication skills? Do you think this is a positive or negative influence?
- How have your life experiences influenced your communication skills? Do you think this is a positive or negative influence?
- What are some consequences of reckless communication have you've experienced?
- How can you start to make some of these healthy communication strategies, habits in your everyday life?

- Do you have any new insights on the connection between controlling your words and your personal relationship with God?

D.I.V.A. CHALLENGE

The D.I.V.A. Challenge for this week is to reread the scriptures in this session, pray and reflect on your current communications style and conversations you engage in. Think about if you are honoring God with your words when it comes to using foul language, engaging in gossip, backbiting, and other areas we've discussed today. Think about what small changes you can begin to implement today so that your conversation glorifies God, and put them into action. Write about it in your handbook.

Tell the girls you will ask them to report on their progress with this challenge at the next session.

CLOSING REFLECTION & PRAYER

Share with the group:

The powerful thing about the human mind is just as we can learn, we can UNLEARN by using some of these new strategies and taking in the instructions provided in scripture. By 'taming our tongues" and aiming to let our words be pleasing to our Heavenly Father, we position ourselves to let our light shine for Him.

Invite a girl to pray out loud for the group based on the topic discussed. End the session with this prayer:

Father, thank you for your word, which acts a light to our feet. Forgive us for when we have broken your heart by using words to tear others down. Convict our hearts, and give us a desire to let our words and actions be pleasing to you. Grant us the strength to take the higher road when others test us, and to practice self-control, remembering that our words represent you. Let the words of our mouths be pleasing in your sight.

Session 20 Handout:
Say What?!?! Communication Tips

In a healthy communication exchange there is understanding between those involved, and conflicts are more likely to be resolved. Communication involves speaking and listening.

* Pray and think before speaking.
* Make sure your message is clear and straight to the point.
* Articulate your message – no "mumble mouth."
* Good grammar makes a huge impact.
* Know when to use open-ended and closed questions to get feedback on if your listener is understanding.
* Speak assertively - Hold your head up! Your voice matters!
* Watch your tone! A message said in a calm voice can sound totally different then the same message said in an angry voice.
* When in a conflict, use "I" messages instead of "you" messages.

Using "I" Messages allows you to say how you feel without attacking or blaming the other person.

I FEEL (share your feelings, you can use more than one word): **I feel angry...**

WHEN (state what the person has done to you): **when you change the channel while I'm watching TV...**

BECAUSE (tell why you feel this way): **because it's rude and disrespectful.**

WILL YOU (request what you would like to happen): **Will you ask me if I am finished watching before you change the channel?**

Now, you try it with your own words! I feel _____ when _____ because _____ . Will you _____?

* Actually listen! Thinking about what you are going to say while the other person is talking is NOT listening.
* Take a minute to process the message you have just received before responding. Ask the person to say it again if necessary.
* Encourage the speaker with body language, such as eye contact and head nods, to let them know you are listening and that you understand what they are saying.
* Check to make sure you understand what the speaker is saying by asking questions like "What did you mean..." or "Could you tell me more..." or restate what the speaker said in your own words.
* In a conflict, acknowledge the speaker's feelings, like saying "It sounds like you're really upset" to show that you understand the meaning behind what they are saying.

Session 20 Activity:
Say What?!?! Role-Play Scenarios

Work with your group to discuss how the healthy communication tips can be used in these situations. Develop a role play to present to the group, and consider which scriptures below support your role play.

Scenario 1—You always clash with your parents. You feel like your parents don't trust you, and they never let you do anything. You are getting older and feel they should start treating you like it. Your best friend is having a birthday party and you are about to ask you mom can you go.

Scenario 2—Every since your friend got a boyfriend, she never spends any time with you or your other friends. You think something is wrong with this, and you are going to talk to her about it after school.

Scenario 3—Your teacher always assumes that you are the one that is talking when the class is being disrupted. You feel unfairly treated, and you plan to talk to the teacher about it when class is over.

Scenario 4—You come home from school to find your sister wearing your favorite shirt. She did not ask for your permission to wear it. You got into a big argument the last time she wore your skirt without asking because she returned it with a tear in it. You plan to confront her about this once and for all.

Scenario 5—Your classmates tell you that a girl you've recently befriended has stolen things from several people at school. She's planning to spend the night at your house this weekend, but the rumors give you second thoughts about being her friend. You plan to ask her about the rumors at lunch.

Scriptures to reflect on

Psalms 19:14

Proverbs 16:23-24

Ephesians 4:29-32

2 Timothy 2:22-26

Proverbs 18:13

Proverbs 18:8

Session 21
Say it Loud!

SESSION GOALS:

D.I.V.A. participants will:

- Review scripture and learn about Christ's directives "The Great Commission"
- Develop an understanding of evangelism as the Christian's responsibility and obligation
- Discuss obstacles and methods to share the Gospel of Jesus Christ in their every day lives
- Practice sharing the message of salvation with each other

SCRIPTURE FOCUS:

Matthew 28:16-20 (Message); Romans 3:23; Romans 6:23; John 3:16; Romans 10:9-10; Luke 9:23-26; Matthew 10:17-20 (Message); Matthew 10:12-15 (Message); 1 Corinthians 3:7-9; Isaiah 55:10-11; Matthew 10:5-8 (Message)

MATERIALS NEEDED:

- D.I.V.A. Handbooks, one book for each girl
- Bibles: Inform the girls to bring Bibles if they have them
- S.A.Y. It Loud Cards
- Salvation Illustration from Session Two

PREP TASKS:

- Print the S.A.Y. It Loud Handout on cardstock, print, and cut out so each girl in the group receives a card

----

RECALL (if applicable)

If applicable, follow the directions for facilitating the recall segment described in the introduction on page 18.

CHECK –IN

Make up your own Check-In activity or facilitate the "Highs and Lows" Check-In activity described in the introduction on page 17.

FOUNDATION

Share with the group:

As Christians, we have many responsibilities. Scripture instructs us to love God with all our hearts, and love our brothers and sisters as we love ourselves. We are commanded to praise and worship God, and to serve others with our talents and treasures. Another responsibility, spoken directly from Jesus, is to share the "Good News" or the message of salvation with others. In the Bible, this is called "The Great Commission." This is also called "witnessing" or evangelism. Evangelism is the spreading of the Christian gospel by public speaking or personal witness. In today's session, we will learn about evangelism, and our responsibility to share the Gospel of Jesus Christ.

Ask the group the following questions, "How did you learn about salvation through Jesus Christ? Where were you when you first heard the message of the Gospel, and who told it to you? Do you recall your first thoughts about it? If so, what were they?" Discuss their responses.

Ask someone to read Matthew 28:16-20 (MSG)

Meanwhile, the eleven disciples were on their way to Galilee, headed for the mountain Jesus had set for their reunion. The moment they saw him they worshiped him. Some, though, held back, not sure about worship, about risking themselves totally. Jesus, undeterred, went right ahead and gave his charge: "God authorized and commanded me to commission you: Go out and train everyone you meet, far and near, in this way of life, marking them by baptism in the threefold name: Father, Son, and Holy Spirit. Then instruct them in the practice of all I have commanded you. I'll be with you as you do this, day after day after day, right up to the end of the age."

Share with the group:

After Jesus' death on the cross, He was buried, and then came back to life three days later (Review the Illustration provided in Session 2). Before He went back to heaven, He appeared to his disciples in Galilee and gave them these instructions. This is the last in-person and direct message from Jesus to the disciples that was recorded in the Bible. We are the modern day disciples of Jesus Christ, His followers who believe His word. Since we believe and accept Him, we are called to assist in spreading the message of His love and sacrifice for us. This is one important way we put our faith to action. This is not optional. We are obligated to do so, and witnessing to others is central to our purpose as Christians.

Ask the girls, "What do you think we should share with others when we witness to them? What are the key points to include in the discussion?" Discuss their responses.

Distribute the S.A.Y. cards you have prepared. Tell the girls to follow along as you explain the different components. Answer any questions they have to the best of your ability as you explain it.

Share with the group:

A simple way you can share your faith is by using the S.A.Y. outline to share about salvation in Jesus Christ.

The S is for "see your sin." We all have sinned. No one is perfect. Each of us has a problem the Bible calls sin. The result of sin is spiritual death. Spiritual death means eternal separation from God. We all need salvation. Admit honestly to God that you have sinned and disobeyed Him.

Romans 3:23
For all have sinned and fall short of the glory of God.

Romans 6:23
For the wages of sin is death, but the gift of God is eternal life in Christ Jesus our Lord.

The A is for "Accept Jesus." Accept that Jesus Christ is God's Son. Willingly accept Jesus' gift of forgiveness from sin. God loves each of us, so He offers us salvation through Jesus' death on the cross, burial, and resurrection. Believe in your heart that Jesus died for you, and only through Him you are saved. We have done nothing to deserve His love and salvation.

John 3:16
For God so loved the world that he gave his one and only Son, that whoever believes in him shall not perish but have eternal life.

Y is for "You confess it." Confess your faith in Jesus Christ as Savior and Lord with your mouth. YOU must do this for yourself. It is a personal decision. After you have received Jesus Christ into your life, share your decision with another person. Tell your pastor or a Christian friend about your decision. Following Christ's example, ask for baptism by immersion in your local church as a public expression of your faith.

Romans 10:9-10
If you confess with your mouth, 'Jesus is Lord,' and believe in your heart that God raised him from the dead, you will be saved. For it is with your heart that you believe and are justified, and it is with your mouth that you confess and are saved.

Here are a few tips to help you as you share this message:

- Pray for courage and wisdom before speaking.
- Be yourself! Be real. Share your spiritual journey.
- Use the S.A.Y. outline as a guide and not a script.
- After you share, ask them to trust in Christ with a prayer in their own words if they believe.
- Invite them to church, Bible study or your D.I.V.A. group (if they are a girl).
- Keep in touch with them, if possible, to help encourage them as new believers in the faith.

Ask the girls the following questions, "So if we know that God has commanded us to share the Gospel, why don't we share it? What obstacles keep you from sharing your faith?" Responses may include being embarrassed, viewing witnessing as an adult activity, not knowing what to say, feeling like they don't know enough (being asked a question and not knowing the answer), fear of rejection (the person not accepting what they have to say), etc. Discuss their responses.

Ask for volunteers to read the following scriptures:

Luke 9:23-26
Then he said to them all: "Whoever wants to be my disciple must deny themselves and take up their cross daily and follow

160

me. For whoever wants to save their life will lose it, but whoever loses their life for me will save it. What good is it for someone to gain the whole world, and yet lose or forfeit their very self? Whoever is ashamed of me and my words, the Son of Man will be ashamed of them when he comes in his glory and in the glory of the Father and of the holy angels.

Matthew 10:17-20 (MSG)
Don't be naive. Some people will impugn your motives, others will smear your reputation—just because you believe in me. Don't be upset when they haul you before the civil authorities. Without knowing it, they've done you—and me—a favor, given you a platform for preaching the kingdom news! And don't worry about what you'll say or how you'll say it. The right words will be there; the Spirit of your Father will supply the words.

Share with the group:

Witnessing to others is not an easy task. It requires us to open up and show our faith to others. We may be afraid that people will talk about us or that our reputation will suffer if people know that we are Christians. The scripture above tell us not to be naïve about it. Some people will not like you because you are a Christian. Jesus also clearly states that if we are ashamed to claim Him, He will be ashamed to claim us. And I don't know about you, but I need God in my corner everyday! I can't afford for Him not to be there for me! Being connected and having eternal life with God outweighs any "haters" we may encounter because of our faith. If we put it in perspective, we are really blessed to have the freedom to share our faith. There are places in the world today

where people can be killed for sharing the Christian faith. Let's not take it for granted. The great news is that we are not alone, Jesus promises to be with us every step of the way.

Ask the girls the following questions, "What if they don't accept what you have to say? How will you handle it? What responsibility do you think you have at this point to continue to share?" Discuss their responses.

Ask for volunteers to read the following scriptures:

Matthew 10:12-15 (MSG)
When you knock on a door, be courteous in your greeting. If they welcome you, be gentle in your conversation. If they don't welcome you, quietly withdraw. Don't make a scene. Shrug your shoulders and be on your way. You can be sure that on Judgment Day they'll be mighty sorry—but it's no concern of yours now.

1 Corinthians 3:7-9
So neither the one who plants nor the one who waters is anything, but only God, who makes things grow. The one who plants and the one who waters have one purpose, and they will each be rewarded according to their own labor. For we are co-workers in God's service; you are God's field, God's building.

Isaiah 55:10-11
As the rain and the snow come down from heaven, and do not return to it without watering the earth and making it bud and flourish, so that it yields seed for the sower and bread for the eater, so is my word that goes out from my mouth: It will not return to me empty, but will

accomplish what I desire and achieve the purpose for which I sent it.

Share with the group:

It is not our job to make people accept Jesus Christ. The scripture tells us to be nice and respectful, and not force ourselves or our message onto others. Our job is just to share the message or to plant the seed. Another believer may come along and plant another seed at a later time that may help them make a decision. God will draw them to Him. If they refuse to listen, or say they are not interested, that is okay. Don't take it personally. The scripture tells us to back off and leave them alone. They are not rejecting you, they are rejecting Jesus. The scripture also indicates that God's word will not return to him without working in the way He intended it. After you walk away, continue to pray for them on your own.

Ask a girl to read Matthew 10:5-8 (MSG)
Jesus sent his twelve harvest hands out with this charge: "Don't begin by traveling to some far-off place to convert unbelievers. And don't try to be dramatic by tackling some public enemy. Go to the lost, confused people right here in the neighborhood. Tell them that the kingdom is here. Bring health to the sick. Raise the dead. Touch the untouchables. Kick out the demons. You have been treated generously, so live generously.

Share with the group:

There are several styles of evangelism. You will most likely engage the most in witnessing to those who you already have a relationship with. This includes friends, families, and others you have access to in school and your community. The scripture indicates that you can start to share your faith right where you are, with people you already know. Be mindful that your behavior and attitude affects your witness and people's ability to receive the Gospel from you. Live your faith and it makes it easier to enter into conversation about it. Because you know the people, don't use this as an excuse to put off sharing the Gospel for a later time. You may have the opportunity to witness to a stranger in the grocery store, at work, on the bus stop, or any other public place.

ACTIVITY: S.A.Y. It Loud!

Divide the girls into pairs. Tell them to each come up with a real person that they could share their faith with, and tell them to give a few details about the person to their partner. Using the S.A.Y. Outline, the girls will take turns sharing their S.A.Y. Outline with their partners. The partner should use the details shared about the person to respond to the S.A.Y. Outline (accept, reject, ask questions, etc.). Encourage the girls to take the exercise seriously, and to act as if this were a real opportunity to witness to someone else. If time allows, have the girls switch partners and try the S.A.Y. Outline again with a different person in mind.

Ask for a few pairs to volunteer to act out their conversation for the group. Discuss any particular strategies the girls used to share their faith. Make suggestions as appropriate.

DISCUSSION

Based on the activity and the scriptures read, lead the girls in a discussion using the following prompts:

- On a scale of 1-10, how comfortable do you feel with sharing the S.A.Y. Outline with someone in real life? What would increase your confidence in sharing the outline?
- What personality traits do you have that may be useful to you as you share your faith with others?
- What are your biggest obstacles to sharing the Gospel of Jesus Christ? What can you do to overcome them?
- What areas in your life may be negatively affecting your ability to witness to others? What can you do to improve those areas?
- Name three people you can share your faith with. How will you start the conversation with them?
- Please share any new insights you have on sharing your faith.

D.I.V.A. CHALLENGE

The D.I.V.A. Challenge for this week is to reread the S.A.Y. outline and attempt to memorize the points covered on the S.A.Y. card you received. Plan to share the Gospel of Jesus Christ using the S.A.Y. outline with at least one person this week. Write about it in your handbook.

Tell the girls you will ask them to report on their progress with this challenge at the next session.

CLOSING REFLECTION & PRAYER

Share with the group:

As disciples of Jesus Christ, we are obligated to share the message with others so that everyone would have the opportunity to accept the gift of eternal life through Jesus Christ. Although it may be awkward or uncomfortable at times, our reward is in being obedient to God. We also can take pleasure in knowing that God used us to draw someone to Him. When the Holy Spirit sets you up for an opportunity, take it. Don't just walk away. Don't do it just because it's wrong if you don't, but because your choice to obey (or disobey) can change someone's life forever.

Invite a girl to pray out loud for the group based on the topic discussed. End the session with this prayer:

Lord Jesus, thank you for your gift of salvation. Make us aware when opportunities arise to share our faith. Give us wisdom and courage to say the right words, and to respond to questions others may have. Let your Holy Spirit speak through us. Help us to let our witness, demeanor, and words communicate your love. Help us to grow in our own faith and understanding, so we may fully understand the sacrifice you made for us through your death, burial, and resurrection. Increase our desire to share the Gospel. Use us for your glory.

S.A.Y. It Loud!
Session 21 -Sharing Our Faith

S-See Your Sin

We all have sinned. No one is perfect. Admit honestly to God that you have sinned and disobeyed Him.
Romans 3:23; Romans 6:23

A-Accept Jesus

Accept that Jesus died for you, and only through Him are you saved. Willingly accept His gift of forgiveness from sin.
John 3:16

Y-You Confess It

Confess your faith in Jesus Christ as your Lord and Savior with your mouth. You must make this decision for yourself.
Romans 10:9-10

Tips

* Pray for courage and wisdom
* Be yourself! Share your spiritual journey
* Ask them to trust in Christ with a prayer in their own words if they believe
* Invite them to church or bible study
* Keep in touch if possible

From Destined D.I.V.A. © 2012 Laura E. Knights

S.A.Y. It Loud!
Session 21 -Sharing Our Faith

S-See Your Sin

We all have sinned. No one is perfect. Admit honestly to God that you have sinned and disobeyed Him.
Romans 3:23; Romans 6:23

A-Accept Jesus

Accept that Jesus died for you, and only through Him are you saved. Willingly accept His gift of forgiveness from sin.
John 3:16

Y-You Confess It

Confess your faith in Jesus Christ as your Lord and Savior with your mouth. You must make this decision for yourself.
Romans 10:9-10

Tips

* Pray for courage and wisdom
* Be yourself! Share your spiritual journey
* Ask them to trust in Christ with a prayer in their own words if they believe
* Invite them to church or bible study
* Keep in touch if possible

From Destined D.I.V.A. © 2012 Laura E. Knights

S.A.Y. It Loud!
Session 21 -Sharing Our Faith

S-See Your Sin

We all have sinned. No one is perfect. Admit honestly to God that you have sinned and disobeyed Him.
Romans 3:23; Romans 6:23

A-Accept Jesus

Accept that Jesus died for you, and only through Him are you saved. Willingly accept His gift of forgiveness from sin.
John 3:16

Y-You Confess It

Confess your faith in Jesus Christ as your Lord and Savior with your mouth. You must make this decision for yourself.
Romans 10:9-10

Tips

* Pray for courage and wisdom
* Be yourself! Share your spiritual journey
* Ask them to trust in Christ with a prayer in their own words if they believe
* Invite them to church or bible study
* Keep in touch if possible

From Destined D.I.V.A. © 2012 Laura E. Knights

S.A.Y. It Loud!
Session 21 -Sharing Our Faith

S-See Your Sin

We all have sinned. No one is perfect. Admit honestly to God that you have sinned and disobeyed Him.
Romans 3:23; Romans 6:23

A-Accept Jesus

Accept that Jesus died for you, and only through Him are you saved. Willingly accept His gift of forgiveness from sin.
John 3:16

Y-You Confess It

Confess your faith in Jesus Christ as your Lord and Savior with your mouth. You must make this decision for yourself.
Romans 10:9-10

Tips

* Pray for courage and wisdom
* Be yourself! Share your spiritual journey
* Ask them to trust in Christ with a prayer in their own words if they believe
* Invite them to church or bible study
* Keep in touch if possible

From Destined D.I.V.A. © 2012 Laura E. Knights

Session 22

Give Thanks, Give Back

SESSION GOALS:

D.I.V.A. participants will:

- Review the scriptural context of service as a Christian responsibility
- Discuss the "attitude of service" described in scripture
- Plan a sample service project to address community needs
- Reflect on their lives as an opportunity to practice daily service

SCRIPTURE FOCUS:

1 Corinthians 13:3-7; Matthew 22:37-40; 1 John 4:19-21; James 2:14-17; James 2:24; Matthew 25:35-40; Matthew 7:12 (Message); 2 Corinthians 9:7; Matthew 6:1-4 (Message); Colossians 3:23-24; 1 Peter 4:8-11

MATERIALS NEEDED:

- D.I.V.A. Handbooks, one book for each girl
- Bibles: Inform the girls to bring Bibles if they have them
- Flip Chart Paper (approximately 8-10 sheets)
- Markers
- Pens (One for each girl)
- Service Brainstorm Activity Worksheet

PREP TASKS:

- Copy the "Service Brainstorm" Activity Worksheet (one per girl)
- Recreate the Service illustration on the newsprint paper and post so everyone can see it
- Write each of these phrase on a separate sheet of fiip chart paper: "Why we serve" and "An attitude of service"

RECALL (if applicable)

If applicable, follow the directions for facilitating the recall segment described in the introduction on page 18.

CHECK –IN

Make up your own Check-In activity or facilitate the "Highs and Lows" Check-In activity described in the introduction on page 17.

FOUNDATION

Share with the group:

As a child of God, you are in a position to share the love of Christ with others through serving others. Service can take on many different forms. This includes ongoing service through your church or other community organization, such as serving as part of the food ministry or volunteering at a senior citizen home. As you get older and begin to make decisions about your educational and career path, you may choose a service-oriented career such as ministry, social work, a health-related career, or the military, in which service will be an important part of your life and work. Today we will discuss the various ways we can serve others.

Ask the girls the following questions: "What ways do you serve others? Where do you serve others? Why do you think we should serve others?" Discuss their responses.

Ask for volunteers to read the following scriptures:

1 Corinthians 13:3-7
If I give all I possess to the poor and give over my body to hardship that I may boast, but do not have love, I gain nothing. Love is patient, love is kind. It does not envy, it does not boast, it is not proud. It does not dishonor others, it is not self-seeking, it is not easily angered, it keeps no record of wrongs. Love does not delight in evil but rejoices with the truth. It always protects, always trusts, always hopes, always perseveres.

Matthew 22:37-40
Jesus replied: "'Love the Lord your God with all your heart and with all your soul and with all your mind.' This is the first and greatest commandment. And the second is like it: 'Love your neighbor as yourself.' All the Law and the Prophets hang on these two commandments."

1 John 4:19-21
We love because he first loved us. Whoever claims to love God yet hates a brother or sister is a liar. For whoever does not love their brother and sister, whom they have seen, cannot love God, whom they have not seen. And he has given us this command: Anyone who loves God must also love their brother and sister.

Ask the girls, "What is the connection between these scriptures and service?" Discuss their responses.

Share with the group:

There is a lot of emphasis in the Bible about love—how we express it to God and how we show it to others. From the scripture in 1 Corinthians, we see that love is an action word, attitude, and way of being. We are to love others and treat others just as we would want them to treat us. Another way we serve is through our everyday life—how we treat people, how we talk to them, how we share love, and how we share our faith with others. Service is not just a one- time or special event thing. Love and service go together. God is calling us to live a life of service in every part of our lives—at school, at home, and even in the grocery store! Serving others provides an opportunity for us to show God's love.

Ask the girls the following questions: "In what ways have you experienced God's love? If you look at your life, would you say you are blessed? Why or why not? What are you grateful for?" Discuss their responses.

Share with the group:

The scripture says we love because He loved us first. You may have also heard the common saying, "To whom much is given, much is required." This means that God blesses us with love, joy, peace, health, and even material things. We should share those things with others. People experience God through us.

Ask for volunteers to read the following scriptures:

James 2:14-17
What good is it, my brothers and sisters, if someone claims to have faith but has no deeds? Can such faith save them? Suppose a brother or a sister is without clothes and daily food. If one of you says to them, "Go in peace; keep warm and well fed," but does nothing about their physical needs, what good is it? In the same way, faith by itself, if it is not accompanied by action, is dead.

James 2:24
You see that a person is considered righteous by what they do and not by faith alone.

Share with the group:

Let's be clear. Salvation cannot be earned or maintained by good works. Salvation is only received by accepting and believing that Jesus Christ is Lord and Savior. Once you receive salvation, being righteous means that you are making daily efforts to live according to God's word and standards. It means you are putting your faith to work through serving others. Remember love is an action word! Good works will flow as a result of our salvation.

Ask for volunteers to read the following scriptures:

Matthew 25:35-40
For I was hungry and you gave me something to eat, I was thirsty and you gave me something to drink, I was a stranger and you invited me in, I needed clothes and you clothed me, I was sick and you looked after me, I was in prison and you came to visit me. "Then the righteous will answer him, 'Lord, when did we see you hungry and feed you, or thirsty and give you something to drink? When did we see you a stranger and invite you in, or needing clothes and clothe you? When did we see you sick or in prison and go to visit you?' "The King will reply, 'Truly I tell you, whatever you did for one of the least of these brothers and sisters of mine, you did for me.'

Matthew 7:12 (MSG)
Here is a simple, rule-of-thumb guide for behavior: Ask yourself what you want people to do for you, then grab the initiative and do it for them. Add up God's Law and Prophets and this is what you get.

Share with the group:

The scriptures are clear—when we serve others, we serve God! Jesus said the second greatest commandment was to love others— not in mushy, touch-feely ways, but in concrete ways through our actions. Every action performed out of kindness, powered by the understanding of Christ and His love, is Christian service. The world desperately needs to experience Christians who are willing to show who Christ is with their actions.

Ask the girls the following questions, "Do you have people in your life that are examples of this? How do they show love and serve others? What are some of the characteristics of these people?" Discuss their responses.

Share with the group:

These people could be called servant-leaders. Our Lord and Savior Jesus Christ is our ultimate example of a servant leader. Because of His love for us and His love for God, the Father, He served us by dying for our sins. He serves us by loving us, protecting us, and guiding us each day throughout our lives. God is calling us to be leaders by serving others and helping them find their way to Him. Now that we are clear that service is part of our responsibilities as a Christian, what type of attitude do you think we should have about service? Discuss their responses.

Ask the girls the following questions, "On a scale of 1-10, how would you rate your attitude when it comes to serving others?

What has influenced you to have this attitude about service?" Discuss their responses.

Post a piece of flip chart paper. Ask for volunteers to read the following scriptures. Pause between each scripture and ask the group to name any characteristics that describe the attitude we should have about service based on the scripture read. Write down their responses.

2 Corinthians 9:7
Each of you should give what you have decided in your heart to give, not reluctantly or under compulsion, for God loves a cheerful giver.

Matthew 6: 1-4 (MSG)
Be especially careful when you are trying to be good so that you don't make a performance out of it. It might be good theater, but the God who made you won't be applauding. When you do something for someone else, don't call attention to yourself. You've seen them in action, I'm sure—'play actors' I call them—treating prayer meeting and street corner alike as a stage, acting compassionate as long as someone is watching, playing to the crowds. They get applause, true, but that's all they get. When you help someone out, don't think about how it looks. Just do it—quietly and unobtrusively. That is the way your God, who conceived you in love, working behind the scenes, helps you out.

Colossians 3:23-24
Whatever you do, work at it with all your heart, as working for the Lord, not for human masters, since you know that you

will receive an inheritance from the Lord as a reward. It is the Lord Christ you are serving.

1 Peter 4:8-11
Above all, love each other deeply, because love covers over a multitude of sins. Offer hospitality to one another without grumbling. Each of you should use whatever gift you have received to serve others, as faithful stewards of God's grace in its various forms. If anyone speaks, they should do so as one who speaks the very words of God. If anyone serves, they should do so with the strength God provides, so that in all things God may be praised through Jesus Christ. To him be the glory and the power for ever and ever. Amen.

Re-read all the characteristics the girls identified in the scriptures out loud. Ask the girls if there are any other characteristics they think should be added. Add the following characteristics if they have not been identified by the girls: willing, cheerful, sincere, humble, "giving your all," and respectful.

Ask the group to brainstorm ways they can serve in their daily lives. Write their responses on a piece of flip chart paper. Examples include church ministry work, helping in the community, helping parents with chores around the house, treating teachers with respect, etc. Encourage the girls to think broadly, and to think about all areas of their lives.

ACTIVITY: SERVICE BRAINSTORM

Share with the group:

Service can be project based too. A great opportunity for project-based service is by serving a need in your community. Meaningful service that makes a great impact is where the community's need overlaps with our personal assets. Community refers to any group with a common interest that you belong to. Personal assets are your passions, skills, knowledge, and experience that you can contribute to serve others.

Refer to the service illustration that you have recreated on the flip chart paper.

Ask the girls to identify the different communities they belong to, and write their responses on a piece of flip chart paper. Responses may include the church, schools where the girls attend, their families, a specific neighborhood, etc. Once they have shared their responses, ask them to agree on one community to use for the session activity.

Instruct the girls to think about the community they agreed upon, and to identify any needs the community may have where assistance or improvement is needed. Write their responses on the flip-chart paper.

Instruct the girls to share any personal assets they have that may be used to address some of the community needs on the list. Encourage them to think broadly about the skills and strengths they bring to the table. Write their responses on the flip-chart paper.

Based on the community needs and personal assets discussed by the group, lead them in compiling a list of possible service projects they could do to help in these areas. If you have access to the Internet, they may even want to do a search for service project ideas. Write their responses on the flip-chart paper.

Divide the girls into groups, assign the girls one of the service projects on the list, or tell them to come up with their own project to address a community need. Distribute the Service Brainstorm Activity worksheet, and give each group a sheet of flip chart paper and markers. Tell the girls to answer the questions about their projects as a group, and to select a representative that will report back to the large group. Give each group approximately 15-20 minutes to brainstorm the details for their service project. After each group is finished, bring the large group together so each group representative can share the details of their project.

Ask the girls if there is a project presented that they would like to actually complete as a group. If so, help the girls establish a timeline for planning the project beyond the session time (See D.I.V.A. Challenge section).

DISCUSSION

Based on the activity and the scriptures read, lead the girls in a discussion using the following prompts:

- What inspires you to take action to improve your community?
- What personal assets can you use to serve others?

- Do you think we have an obligation to give back to our communities? Why or why not?
- What can you do to serve your family more?
- What can you do to serve your friends more?
- What can you do to serve more in your church community?
- What can you do to serve more in the neighborhood you live in?

D.I.V.A. CHALLENGE

The D.I.V.A. Challenge for this week is to think of ways you can be of more service in your everyday life. Create a list of 5 service activities, and implement at least one of them this week. Write about it in your handbook.

Tell the girls you will ask them to report on their progress with this challenge at the next session.

OPTIONAL GROUP CHALLENGE:
Continue planning one of the activities the girls came up with during the session. Take a poll to see if they are interested, and allow them to vote on which of the projects they all could work on together. Help the girls facilitate this as a one-time or ongoing service project. To make this meaningful for the girls, allow them to really take charge of the project and serve in a support capacity only. Establish an upcoming meeting or other date for a planning meeting, so the girls can set a timeline and divide the tasks. The Global Youth Service Day website is an excellent resource for youth-led service projects, and the site offers service project ideas, planning guidelines, sample budgets,

and planning templates for youth to plan and facilitate a service project. Visit www.gysd.org/resources for more information.

CLOSING REFLECTION & PRAYER

Share with the group:

Remember service is a way of life! There is a time and place for all types of service— serving in ministry at your church, volunteering with a community organization, helping a family or friend, and treating others with love in your daily life. Service can be a project, but it is not JUST a project. Service is showing God's love to others.

Invite a girl to pray out loud for the group based on the topic discussed. End the session with this prayer:

Lord Jesus, thank you for loving us first. Give us the desire to serve others willingly and cheerfully as an extension of your love in our families, with our friends, in our schools, in our communities, and everywhere that we go. Open our eyes to our skills and talents, and how they may be used for your kingdom. We are so grateful for salvation and all the blessings you have given us, and we understand that our actions of service are a reflection of these gifts. May our heart's desire be not to receive glory for our acts of service, but to genuinely serve you and others. Make us aware of these opportunities to serve each day.

Session 22 Activity:
Service Brainstorm

Work with your group to come up with a service project based on one of the community needs discussed in today's session. Answer the questions below, and write your responses on your flip chart paper.

WHAT
...specifically will you do?

...real community need does this project address

WHO
...will you serve?

...will you need help from?

WHEN
...will you do this?

HOW
...much will this cost?

WHY
...is this important? How will this project impact the community need?

Personal Assets are your passions, skills, knowledge, and experience.

Personal Assets

What do you really enjoy doing?

What strengths and talents do you have that can be used to address a community need?

What issue or causes are you really passionate about?

Service

The Need

A community is any group with a common interest that you belong to.

What inspires you to serve in your community?

What areas do you think need to be addressed or improved in the community?

Where do you think you can make a positive impact?

An opportunity for **meaningful service** exists where the community need and personal assets overlap.

FOCUSED ON THE FUTURE
Sessions 23-25

Theme Overview:

The sessions in this theme encourage the girls to look to their futures with great expectation, and to take steps to reflect and prepare for the road ahead. At the same time, these sessions instruct the girls to be prayerful about their futures, seeking God's Word and will in every aspect of their lives.

This theme covers topics such as planning for the future, college and career exploration, and goal setting. The focus scripture for all sessions in this theme is Jeremiah 29:11:

"For I know the plans I have for you, declares the Lord, plans to prosper you and not to harm you, plans to give you hope and a future."

Through these sessions, girls are reminded that although it is wise and recommended for us to plan for the future, we must remain prayerful that our plans match up with God's plan for our lives.

Session 23

The Road Ahead

SESSION GOALS:

D.I.V.A. participants will:
- Review Bible verses that speak about considering the future
- Understand the connection between our past and what lies ahead
- Complete a dream plan and discuss a vision for their future

SCRIPTURE FOCUS:

Psalm 119:133; Jeremiah 29:11; Ephesians 3:20-21 (Message); Philippians 4:6 (Message); Philippians 3:13-14; Romans 5:3-5 (Message)

MATERIALS NEEDED:

- D.I.V.A. Handbooks, one book for each girl
- Bibles: Inform the girls to bring Bibles if they have them
- Color pencils/Markers
- Pens for each girl
- "My Dream Plan" Activity Worksheet
- "View of the Past" Activity Worksheet

PREP TASKS:

- Copy the "My Dream Plan" Activity Worksheet (one copy per girl)
- Copy the "View of the Past" Activity Worksheet (one copy per girl)

RECALL (if applicable)

If applicable, follow the directions for facilitating the recall segment described in the introduction on page 18.

CHECK –IN

Make up your own Check-In activity or facilitate the "Highs and Lows" Check-In activity described in the introduction on page 17.

FOUNDATION

Share with the group:

Some people think a lot about their future, while others prefer to live in the moment. Whether we have a five-year plan, or we are just trying to make it to the end of the day, God desires that that we seek His will for our lives. The Bible provides instructions to help us deal with whatever the future holds for us —both good and bad. God also prepares us for our future through the triumphs and set backs we have experienced in our past. Today we will talk about our visions for our future and how God is preparing us for the road ahead.

Ask the girls the following questions, "How do you see your future? What do you think lies ahead for you?" Discuss their responses.

ACTIVITY: MY DREAM PLAN

Distribute the "My Dream Plan" Activity Worksheet. Give the girls some time to write their responses, and then as a group, discuss the girls' answers to each question.

Ask the girls, "Do you think the responses you have written on your dream plan line up with what God desires for your life? Do you pray about these areas to get direction from God?" Discuss their responses.

Ask a girl to read Psalm 119:133
Direct my footsteps according to your word; let no sin rule over me.

Share with the group:

God wants us to have great expectations for our future. He also wants us to spend time thinking about how our choices will affect us as we move forward, and for us to be smart about planning out our steps. More importantly, God wants us to consult Him on our future plans through prayer and seeing what the Bible says about every aspect of our lives. When we do this, God will direct our path.

Ask for volunteers to read the following scriptures:

Jeremiah 29:11
For I know the plans I have for you," declares the Lord, "plans to prosper you and not to harm you, plans to give you hope and a future.

Ephesians 3:20
God can do anything, you know—far more than you could ever imagine or guess or request in your wildest dreams! He does it not by pushing us around but by working within us, his Spirit deeply and gently within us. Glory to God in the church! Glory to God in the Messiah, in Jesus! Glory down all the generations! Glory through all millennia! Oh, yes!

Ask the girls the following questions: "How does it feel to know that God has a plan to help you thrive in your future? What do you think about God working to do such great things in your life that you can't even imagine them?" Discuss their responses.

Share with the group:

When we include God in our planning for the future, we can have confidence in His promises to us. However, despite these awesome promises from God, so many people still worry about their future. Some say it is human nature to worry; however, as we grow in our understanding of God and our relationship with Him, we begin to get stronger at living according to His Word. We then can begin to replace our worry with faith in God's will for our lives.

Ask the girls: "Do you think a lot of

teenagers worry about the future? Do you worry about your future? If so, what specifically do you worry about? Do you pray about these areas?" Discuss their responses.

Ask for a volunteer to read Philippians 4:6-7 (MSG)
Don't fret or worry. Instead of worrying, pray. Let petitions and praises shape your worries into prayers, letting God know your concerns. Before you know it, a sense of God's wholeness, everything coming together for good, will come and settle you down. It's wonderful what happens when Christ displaces worry at the center of your life.

Share with the group:

This scripture tells us that instead of worrying about what's going on in our lives or what will happen in the future, we should share our concerns with God in prayer. God may give us an answer or change the situation right away. Other times, the situation may remain the same, but God will help us to change our perspective and give us a sense of peace about the issue. Sometimes we worry about our futures because of things that have happened in the past.

Ask the girls the following questions: "Do you think our past affects our future? How so? Can you provide an example of this?"

Ask for volunteers to read the following scriptures:

Philippians 3:13-14
Brothers and sisters, I do not consider myself yet to have taken hold of it. But one thing I do: Forgetting what is behind and straining toward what is ahead, I press on toward the goal to win the prize for which God has called me heavenward in Christ Jesus.

Romans 5:3-5 (MSG)
There's more to come: We continue to shout our praise even when we're hemmed in with troubles, because we know how troubles can develop passionate patience in us, and how that patience in turn forges the tempered steel of virtue, keeping us alert for whatever God will do next. In alert expectancy such as this, we're never left feeling shortchanged. Quite the contrary —we can't round up enough containers to hold everything God generously pours into our lives through the Holy Spirit!

Share with the group:

Looking at our past is valuable. God uses our good and bad experiences to teach us lessons, build our character, and grow our faith. However, we cannot remain in the past. The scripture tells us to press forward, living for Christ, so God can use our lives as a testimony to his loving kindness toward us. Keeping our eyes on the past for too long can make us miss precious opportunities and lessons God has for us in the future.

ACTIVITY: VIEW OF THE PAST

Share with the group:

A safe driver uses the rearview mirror to stay aware of what's happening on the road. The rearview mirror provides the driver an opportunity to look behind them while they are still moving forward. It can be dangerous to stare into the rearview mirror for too long while driving because it takes the driver's focus off the road ahead. Staring into the rearview mirror instead of just taking occasional glances could lead to a crash. If we apply this same concept to our lives, we understand that staring too long in the "rearview mirror" of our life can also take our focus off the present, and the wonderful things God wants to do in our future. Too much focus on the "rearview mirror" of our lives can cause problems.

Distribute the "View of the Past" Activity Worksheet and the color pencils. Tell the girls to draw words or pictures in the rearview mirror to represent past experiences that may be taking their focus away from the road ahead. Discuss their responses.

Share with the group:

Some side rearview mirrors read, "Warning: Objects may be closer than they appear." This is a warning to tell drivers that what they see in the mirror may not be as close to them as they think. Likewise, in your life, your past experiences may seem very overwhelming, and possibly cast a negative shadow over what God wants to do in your life now.

Tell the girls to write a warning in the space provided about the past experiences in their "rearview mirror." For example, a warning may be, "Those negative things that people said about me are not the truth. I am not what they said about me. I am a child of God."

DISCUSSION

Based on the activity and the scriptures read, lead the girls in a discussion using the following prompts:

- Why do you think some people get off track with their dream plans?
- How would you feel if God had something different in store for you other than what you wrote on your dream plan?
- Are you hopeful about your future? Why or why not?
- Do you think most people pray about their future plans? Why or Why not?
- What role do you play in making your dream plan come pass? What role does God play?
- What can you do to include God in your future planning?
- In what ways can looking back to our past be a good thing? In what ways can it be unhealthy?
- In Philippians 3:13-14 (see above), the Apostle Paul talks about "forgetting what is behind." Is that realistic?
- How do you deal with the painful stuff you see in your "rearview mirror?"
- What are some steps you can take to get your eyes more focused on where you're going and less on where you've been?

D.I.V.A. CHALLENGE

Share with the group:

The D.I.V.A. Challenge for this week is to pray about what you wrote on your dream plan, and find at least one scripture that addresses one of the areas listed. Write about it in your handbook.

Tell the girls you will ask them to report on their progress with this challenge at the next session.

CLOSING REFLECTION & PRAYER

Share with the group:

God wants us to stop worrying about our future and stressing about our past. When we put Jesus in the center of our lives, we build our life plans around God's Word and will for our lives. We can look to the road ahead with great optimism and expectations when we are walking with God.

Invite a girl to pray out loud for the group based on the topic discussed. End the session with this prayer:

Father God, we are so grateful that you care about our future. We know that you have a plan and purpose for each one of us. Help us to learn what your Word says about our lives and our futures. Remind us to pray and include you in our planning. Make us aware of any sinful behaviors and attitudes we have that could threaten your plan for us, so that we can repent and turn away from them. Put people in our lives that will help us move forward and not pull us back. Help us to put worry about the future and stress about the past in its proper place so we can experience the full joy of what the road ahead has for us.

Session 23 Activity:
My Dream Plan

1. In five years, I see myself…

2. My goal is to complete _____ years of school after high school.

3. I see myself in the _____ career field.

4. I would prefer to be married by the age of _____ or I don't really want to be married.

5. I would like to have _____ children.

6. I would like to have my first child at _____ years old.

7. In regards to my health, I would like to be…

8. By age 25 I can see myself…

9. I would like to improve my relationships and be closer with the following people in the future….

10. I would really be proud of myself and my life if…

11. If I maintain my current habits, my chances for achieving my goals are…

12. I see my personal relationship with God growing in the following ways...

Session 23 Activity: View of the Past

What past experiences in your "rearview mirror" are distracting you from focusing on the road ahead? Use words or pictures to draw them in the mirror.

Write your warning here:

Some side rearview mirrors read, "WARNING: Objects may be closer than they appear." What warning would you place on the "rearview mirror" of your life to keep you focused?

Session 24

When I Grow Up

SESSION GOALS:

D.I.V.A. participants will:

- Learn Bible verses related to planning for the future
- Review college and career preparation definitions and key concepts
- Work with a group to review key concepts in a fun activity

SCRIPTURE FOCUS:

Proverbs 3:5-6; Philippians 4:6-7 (NLT); Philippians 4:13; Jeremiah 29:11

MATERIALS NEEDED:

- D.I.V.A. Handbooks, one book for each girl
- Bibles: Inform the girls to bring Bibles if they have them
- Flip chart paper
- Markers
- "Career and College Planning" Handout
- "Silly Group Review" Activity Handout
- Pens for each girl

PREP TASKS:

- Copy the "Career and College Planning" Handout (one per girl)
- Copy the "Silly Group Review" Activity Handout (one per girl)
- Prepare a piece of flip chart paper by drawing a line down the middle. Label the top of the left side "Career," and the top of the right side "Preparation."

RECALL (if applicable)

If applicable, follow the directions for facilitating the recall segment described in the introduction on page 18.

CHECK –IN

Make up your own Check-In activity or facilitate the "Highs and Lows" Check-In activity described in the introduction on page 17.

FOUNDATION

Share with the group:

At your school, your teachers and guidance counselors may already be talking to you about college and asking you about what you want to be when you grow up. Time flies! Before you know it, you will be walking across the stage graduating from high school! Now is a good time to start thinking about what you want to do once you graduate from high school. This most likely will change over the years, and that's okay and it's perfectly normal. Regardless of what you choose to do after high school, God desires that that we seek His will for our lives. Today we will talk about planning for our future education and career plans.

Ask the girls: "What do you want to be when you grow up? What is your dream career?" Discuss their responses, and write them on the left side of the flip chart paper you have prepared under "Careers."

Ask the girls: "Why are you interested in this career? What preparation do you think is necessary to have this career one day?" Discuss their responses, and write them on the right side of the flip chart paper you have prepared under "Preparation."

Ask for volunteers to read the following scriptures:

Jeremiah 29:11
**For I know the plans I have for you,"
declares the Lord, "plans to prosper you
and not to harm you, plans to give you
hope and a future.**

Proverbs 3:5-6
**Trust in the Lord with all your heart
and lean not on your own understanding;
in all your ways submit to him,
and he will make your paths straight.**

Share with the group:

God promises us that He has great things in store for us when we place Him at the center of our lives. He promises to "make our paths straight" and give us understanding about His will for us in every area of our lives, including our career paths.

Ask the girls the following questions: "Do you think your personal relationship with God affects your career and education goals? Why or why not?" Discuss their responses.

Share with the group

God gives us gifts and talents to use for Him and to serve others. In your quiet time with God, pray for God to show you your unique talents and strengths. These areas should be considered when you think about your future career and the education and preparation required for them.

Ask the group the following questions: "Do you think it will be hard for you to accomplish your career goals? Why or Why not? What are some concerns you have about not accomplishing your career goals?" Discuss their responses.

Ask for volunteers to read the following scriptures:

Philippians 4:6-7 (NLT)

Don't worry about anything; instead, pray about everything. Tell God what you need, and thank him for all he has done. Then you will experience God's peace, which exceeds anything we can understand. His peace will guard your hearts and minds as you live in Christ Jesus.

Philippians 4:13

I can do all this through him who gives me strength.

Share with the group

Although accomplishing our career and educational goals won't necessarily be easy, scripture instructs us not to be stressed about it. Instead, we should pray about it, ask for direction, and receive God's peace as we grow and move closer towards our future. As children of God, we can do anything we put our mind to if we keep Jesus at the center!

Share with the group:

Let's review some information that will help you as you make education and career plans. It is a lot of information, but don't worry about trying to remember everything right now. We will do a fun group activity to help us review the material.

Distribute the "Career and College Planning" Handout. Review and discuss the information on the handout. Answer any questions from the girls to the best of your ability. If there are specific questions that you cannot answer, tell the girls you will research the answer or resources (websites, other people to talk to, etc.) to help them find the answer, and get back to them at a later time.

ACTIVITY: SILLY GROUP REVIEW

Distribute the "Silly Group Review" Activity Handout. Divide the girls into groups of four. Assign the groups a group number (1-4) that corresponds to the prompts on the handout. Explain to the girls that they should work within their groups to discuss and present the key topic area assigned to their group, and then report back to the large group. Give the groups about 10 minutes to create their presentations. As each group presents their information, review the topic areas included in their presentation to make sure everyone understands it. Provide clarification as needed.

DISCUSSION

Based on the activity and the scriptures read, lead the girls in a discussion using the following prompts:

- Did you learn anything new today about preparing for college or a career? If so, what did you learn?
- What's one thing you can start to do now to prepare for your future educational or career plans?
- In your opinion, what does your future college or career plans have to do with your personal relationship with God?
- What obstacles could prevent you from accomplishing your career goals? How can you address these obstacles?
- What additional information do you need about your desired career path?

How can you get the information?
Who can help you?

- What do you think your next steps are for preparing for these goals?
- Who are the adults that will support you as you strive for these goals?

D.I.V.A. CHALLENGE

Share with the group:

The D.I.V.A. Challenge for this week is to pray about the careers you are interested in, and the preparation they require. Visit the website, www.mynextmove.org, type in your dream career, then pick one of the specific jobs on the list. Learn more about the job duties of the position, as well as the education and skills required for the job. Write about it in your handbook.

Tell the girls you will ask them to report on their progress with this challenge at the next session.

CLOSING REFLECTION & PRAYER

Share with the group:

Scripture tells us we can do all things through Jesus Christ who strengthens us. God desires great things for us in our future and in our career, education, and all other areas of our lives! Our future accomplishments in our careers and educational paths are another reason to give God glory for His grace and mercy towards us. Taking time to prepare for our future helps to move us closer in this direction.

Invite a girl to pray out loud for the group based on the topic discussed. End the session with this prayer:

Lord Jesus, thank you for caring about every part of our lives including our future education and career paths. We trust you, and even as we research and prepare for our futures, we still put our faith in you. Order our steps Lord. Reveal to us our unique strengths and skills that should be considered as we plan for the future. Show us the way to go, and give us direction in all our plans so that our lives may give you glory. We will continue to praise you along the way as we experience the blessings you have in store for us.

Career Exploration

It's never too early to start thinking about your future! Take some time to explore different careers that may be of interest to you. Consider your skills, personality, and interests when thinking about a career that you might want in the future. Many people do an assessment survey that asks them questions about themselves to suggest potential career paths they may be interested in. It's important to research and explore so you will know what type of education and other preparation you need for your chosen career. See the websites below for more info.

CAREER EXPLORATION TIPS:

- Talk to your guidance counselor at school about career exploration programs your school offers
- Ask to job-shadow or intern with an adult that works in a job you are interested in
- Write down careers you are interested in and research them at the library or online.
- Start planning for college and other education options now

CHECK OUT THESE CAREER EXPLORATION WEBSITES:

- www.mynextmove.org
- www.driveofyourlife.org
- www.careernoodle.com
- www.careeronestop.org (click "Explore Careers")
- careerservices.rutgers.edu/PCCPmain.shtml
- www.onetonline.org

 ## School Options after High School

FOUR YEAR COLLEGES & UNIVERSITIES

- Prepares students for variety of careers
- Provide opportunities to develop broad learning and transferable skills such as communication skills, critical thinking, research, and writing
- Application process is usually more in-depth, and requires ACT/SAT scores, essay, references, etc.
- Tuition is often more expensive than other school options; tuition at state schools costs less for residents than private schools
- Some degrees offered include Criminal Justice, Business Administration, Behavioral Science, Social Work, Elementary Education, etc.
- Offers Bachelor Degrees and Masters degrees

TWO YEAR COLLEGES

- Also called community college, junior college, or city college
- Prepares students for certain careers or to enroll in a four-year college
- Application requirements are not as strict as four year colleges
- ACT/SAT not required, but a placement test is usually needed to enroll
- More affordable tuition
- Some of the programs offered include Nursing, Radiology, Mortuary Sciences, Emergency Medical Technician, etc.
- Offer certificates and Associate degrees

TECHNICAL & TRADE SCHOOLS

- Also called vocational schools or institutes
- Focused on education and training for specific jobs, such as Pharmacy Technician, Massage Therapy, Medical Assistant, Cosmetology, Medical Billing & Coding, Culinary Arts, etc.
- Prepares students for the state licensing exam for the specific field
- Do not offer college degrees, and some colleges may not accept coursework from these programs if you plan to transfer
- Offer diplomas and certificates; most programs are short-term (3-18 months)

COLLEGE TIPS:

- School costs money! Research and find out how much it costs to attend schools you are interested in.
- Start early to research scholarships and grants (free money) so you will need less loans (money you pay back) for school
- Research to find out the application deadlines and requirements early, so you won't miss important deadlines
- Get help from an adult who is familiar with the process of applying to school.

CHECK OUT THESE WEBSITES:

- www.fafsa.ed.gov (Free Application for Federal Student Aid application)
- nces.ed.gov/collegenavigator (Search engines for all three types of schools)
- studentaid.ed.gov (Federal Student Aid website)
- www.fastweb.com (Search for scholarships)
- www.act.org (Info about the ACT test)
- Sat.collegeboard.org (Info about the SAT test)

Session 24 Activity:
Silly Group Review

DIRECTIONS: Complete the instructions in the box for your assigned group. Be sure to include the key information in your presentation. Use the "Career and College Planning" sheet to help you. Feel free to add any additional information you know.

GROUP 1: Present the key information as a TV commercial. Include a catchy phrase to help us remember.

KEY INFORMATION: Career exploration overview & tips

GROUP 2: Present the key information as a news broadcast. Include a "this just in" special report.

KEY INFORMATION: Four year colleges & universities

GROUP 3: Present the answers in a song or as the theme song from a television show. Try to rhyme.

KEY INFORMATION: Two year colleges

GROUP 4: Present the answers below as a children's story. Begin the story with "Once upon a time..." Include special effect sounds and characters.

KEY INFORMATION: Technical & trade schools

Session 25

Write the Vision

SESSION GOALS:

D.I.V.A. participants will:
- Learn Bible verses related to planning for the future
- Review the SMART goal setting process
- Practice writing short and long-term SMART goals

SCRIPTURE FOCUS:

Jeremiah 29:11; Romans 8:28; Proverbs 22:4 (Message); Psalms 1:1-3; James 4:13-15 (Message); Habakkuk 2:2-4 (Message); Ephesians 3:20-21

MATERIALS NEEDED:

- D.I.V.A. Handbooks, one book for each girl
- Bibles: Inform the girls to bring Bibles if they have them Pens for each girl
- Flip chart paper
- Markers
- "Write the Vision!" Activity Worksheet

PREP TASKS:

- Copy the "Write the Vision!" Activity Worksheet (one copy per girl)
- Write the SMART goal acronym on a sheet a flipchart paper with a brief explanation of each letter. See the "Write the Vision!" Activity Worksheet for prompts. Do not post this sign until instructed to do so in the session outline.

RECALL (if applicable)

If applicable, follow the directions for facilitating the recall segment described in the introduction on page 18.

CHECK –IN

Make up your own Check-In activity or facilitate the "Highs and Lows" Check-In activity described in the introduction on page 17.

FOUNDATION

Share with the group

Previous sessions in the Destined D.I.V.A. Leader's Guide have covered thinking about the future, college and career exploration, and planning for the future. Today, we will discuss creating goals and action plans to help us make these dreams come true. It is a good thing to reflect on your future, and set goals to plan. However, as we have discussed before, God desires that we seek His Word and His will to inform our plans. Prayer, reading God's word, and setting goals and actions steps are a powerful combination to help us see our dreams become reality one day. Today we will talk about how to write goals and action steps for our future plans.

Ask the girls the following questions: "What's a goal you've set for yourself in the past? Were you successful at accomplishing that goal? Why or why not?" Discuss their responses.

Ask for volunteers to read the following scriptures:

Jeremiah 29:11
For I know the plans I have for you, declares the Lord, plans to prosper you and not to harm you, plans to give you hope and a future.

Romans 8:28
And we know that in all things God works for the good of those who love him, who have been called according to his purpose.

Proverbs 22:4 (MSG)
The payoff for meekness and Fear-of-God is plenty and honor and a satisfying life.

Psalms 1:1-3
Blessed is the one who doesn't not walk in step with the wicked or stand in the way that sinners take or sit in the company of mockers, but whose delight in in the law of the Lord, and who meditates on his law day and night. That person is like a tree planted by streams of water, which yields its fruit in season and whose leaf does not wither—whatever they do prospers.

Ask the group the following questions: "What is your measure of success for your life? How does your measure of success line up with God's view of success? What do you think it means to be "called according to his purpose?" Discuss their responses.

Share with the group:

These scriptures show us that God desires for us to be successful in our future. There are different measures of success. For some, success means being rich and famous. For others, it may mean having a good job to take care of their families one day. Neither one of those measures of success are necessarily right or wrong. However, as Christians our ultimate success is that our lives match God's Word. Proverbs 22:4 tells us that the payoff for respecting God and His Word is a life filled with honor and satisfaction. Psalms 1:1-3 shows us that God will make us prosperous in WHATEVER we do when we let our light shine and follow His Word in our actions and words. That sounds like success to me!

Ask for volunteers to read the following scriptures:

James 4:13-15 (MSG)
And now I have a word for you who brashly announce, "Today—at the latest, tomorrow—we're off to such and such a city for the year. We're going to start a business and make a lot of money." You don't know the first thing about tomorrow. You're nothing but a wisp of fog, catching a brief bit of sun before disappearing. Instead, make it a habit to say, "If the Master wills it and we're still alive, we'll do this or that."

Ephesians 3:20-21
Now to him who is able to do immeasurably more than all we ask or imagine, according to his power that is at work within us, to him be glory in the church and in Christ Jesus throughout all generations, for ever and ever! Amen

Share with the group:

If we continue to walk with Him, God promises us that we will experience a beautiful life in the future ahead. God will bless us in all areas of our lives, and those blessings will be according to HIS measure of success. These scriptures caution us to remember who is ultimately responsible for the blessing—God. It is natural and a good thing to be proud of yourself when you accomplish something in your life. However, we must remember that ALL our blessings and success in life are possible because of God's grace and mercy, and Jesus' sacrifice for us on the cross. Even as we create plans and write goals, we must remember to go to God in prayer about those plans. And once

we start seeing our goals come to life, we must give HIM the glory.

Ask a girl to read Habakkuk 2:2-4 (MSG)
And then God answered: "Write this. Write what you see. Write it out in big block letters so that it can be read on the run. This vision-message is a witness pointing to what's coming. It aches for the coming—it can hardly wait! And it doesn't lie. If it seems slow in coming, wait. It's on its way. It will come right on time. "Look at that man, bloated by self-importance—full of himself but soul-empty. But the person in right standing before God through loyal and steady believing is fully alive, really alive.

Share with the group

As your relationship with God strengthens, and you begin to pray and read your Bible more, God will begin to confirm things to you about your life and your future plans. This scripture is telling Habakkuk to "write the vision and make it clear so others can understand it." The vision that scripture is referring to here is God's Word that will come to pass. When we align our goals with God's Word, we can begin to write a vision for our future. Goal setting is one way we can do this.

Ask the girls: "Do any of the scriptures we've read today encourage you in any goals you are striving to achieve? If so, which scripture(s)?" Discuss their responses.

Share with the group

One way we can begin to create goals for the future is by using the SMART goal process. The SMART goal formula has been around for the last 30 years, and has been adapted by many people. When goal setting, think of your goals as a blueprint that not only define the goal, but also define specific action steps you can take to achieve it.

Post the prepared sheet of flip chart paper, and review the acronym using the prompts below.

A SMART goal is…
- S- Specific. Say exactly what you want to achieve
- M-Measurable. Include a measure, so you know if you are on track. Questions to ask yourself are: When? How much? How will we know?
- A – Achievable. Can you reasonably complete this? What will you need help with to accomplish the goal?
- R- Relevant. Does the goal fit with my life right now?
- T- Time-based. What's the deadline? "One day" doesn't work. You must put some timelines on your goals. It's okay if you need to adjust them later.

Walk through the SMART acronym using the goal of getting an "A" in math class. Ask the girls for a response for each letter in the SMART goal steps. Use the prompts on the "Write the Vision!" Activity Worksheet to walk the girls through each step. The final goal may read something like, "Get an "A" in my Advanced Algebra class by the end of the fall semester." When considering if the goal is "achievable," share with the girls that it is important to be realistic. For example, if it's one week before the end of the semester and the student has an "F" in the class, setting a goal to get an "A" by the end of

the semester is not realistic. Suggest that a better option might be for the student to work really hard and aim for a "C" by requesting extra credit and attempting to ace the final exam. The student can then set a new goal to get an "A" for the next semester.

ACTIVITY: WRITE THE VISION!

Distribute the Write the Vision! Activity Worksheet. Give the girls time to practice writing a SMART goal by themselves. Instruct them to write a goal in the "draft goal" space at the top and walk through the SMART goal prompts to clarify their goal. Then, they will re-write the final SMART goal in the space provided at the bottom. After trying it on their own, tell the girls to get with a partner. The girls should take turns reviewing their goal with their partner, and give each other feedback and suggestions about making the goal SMART. The girls can continue to update their goal based on the feedback from their partner. Bring the girls back into the large group, review some of the goals they wrote down, and provide comments as appropriate to help them sharpen their goal.

Share with the group

Now that we have written our goals, the next step is to create action steps. An action step is a specific action that someone could "see" you doing. Action steps are so concrete that if someone asked if you completed it, you should only be able to respond with yes or no as an answer. We want to be direct when writing our action goals, and stay away from "loosey-goosey" action steps. Action steps are a very important step in accomplishing your goals.

Return to the math example discussed above. Ask the girls, "What are some specific action steps we can take to get an "A" in this class?" Discuss their responses. Possible specific action steps include:

- Studying three times per week for an hour each time (note how that is more specific than "studying more" and how someone could "see" them sitting down and studying three times during the week)
- Scheduling afterschool tutoring with the teacher on Tuesday and Thursday
- Turning off the television while doing homework to increase focus
- Preparing clothes and lunch the night before for the next school day to prevent tardiness to school (assuming tardiness negatively affects the grade)
- Turning in each homework assignment on time
- Requesting and completing extra credit assignments from the teacher
- Starting a study group with some of their peers from the math class

Instruct the girls to turn their SMART goal worksheets over and write three specific action steps for their goals. Encourage them to work with a partner to brainstorm possible action steps. Ask for a few volunteers to share the action steps to their goals. Provide assistance as necessary.

DISCUSSION

Based on the activity and the scriptures read, lead the girls in a discussion using the following prompts:

- Did you learn anything new today that changed the way you think about your goals? Have your thoughts about success changed?
- What goals can you make about improving your personal relationship with God (i.e. praying and reading the Bible more, changing behavior, etc.)?
- What other areas of your life do you want to write goals about?
- What support or resources do you need to accomplish your goals? How will you get them?
- What obstacles might you encounter? How will you deal with them?

D.I.V.A. CHALLENGE

Share with the group:

The D.I.V.A. Challenge is to write two goals using the SMART format with action steps for each goal. The goals can be short-term (completed in 0-6 months) or long-term (completed in more than a year) goals. One of these goals should be related to improving your personal relationship with God. After writing your goals, share them with someone who supports you so they can hold you accountable as you try and accomplish the goals. Write about it in your handbook.

Tell the girls you will ask them to report on their progress with this challenge at the next session.

CLOSING REFLECTION & PRAYER

Share with the group:

Scripture provides instructions on God's measure of success, and we are able to create goals for our lives that fall in line with this. God desires to bless us in all areas of our lives, so that we may give Him glory. Writing goals and action steps gives us a blueprint to follow as we move closer to accomplishing our goals.

Invite a girl to pray out loud for the group based on the topic discussed. End the session with this prayer:

Father, thank you for your Word and direction. Thank you for all Your blessings, both the ones we have experienced and those that are still to come. Help us to keep You at the center of all our plans and goals. Give us the desire to please You, so that our measure of success matches Yours. Help us to learn Your word and hide it in our hearts, so that we may apply it to every part of our lives. We are excited for the plans You have for us ahead. Help us to stay close to You so that we may experience every good thing You have for us. Thank You Lord for your goodness and mercy towards us!

Writing SMART Goals Worksheet

D.I.V.A.

Draft Goal: _____

	Your Answers	With Feedback from a Friend
Specific • What EXACTLY do you want to achieve? (Consider who, what, when, why, how)		
Measurable • How will you know if you are on track? • How can you measure progress?		
Achievable • Do you have the skills needed? If not, can you learn them? • What resources/support do you need? • Will the environment around you help or hurt goal achievement? • Can you give the right amount of effort?		
Relevant • Does the goal fit with your life right now? • Is the time right for this?		
Time-bound • What is the deadline? Is it realistic?		

Final Goal: _____

FORMS & TEMPLATES*

*Note: These forms only serve as templates. Please check with the appropriate representative from your church or organization to have the contents tailored for your specific needs. A PDF version of these forms are available in the Destined D.I.V.A. Leader Resource area at www.thedestineddivas.com.

- ✤ D.I.V.A. Roster Template

- ✤ Participation Waiver & Image Release From (Parent Permission Form)

- ✤ D.I.V.A. Outreach Card

- ✤ Donation Request Letter

- ✤ Outing Waiver & Transportation Release

- ✤ D.I.V.A Dollars

Destined D.I.V.A. Group Roster

Name	D.O.B	Phone Number	Email	Parent Name	Parent Phone

Participation Waiver & Image Release

Church/Organization: _____

Date: _____

To: Parent/Guardian of _____

Your teen has been invited to participate in the Destined D.I.V.A. group at our church/organization. Destined D.I.V.A. is a bible study group for girls, ages 13-18, with a focus on teaching life skills and biblical truths that will help young women make positive decisions that are aligned with their identity as children of God. The D.I.V.A. acronym stands for Daughters of Integrity, Virtue, and Anointing. In addition to in bible studies, the girls are also educated on life skill issues such as self-esteem, healthy relationships, sexual purity, goal setting, anger management, leadership, stress management, and several other topics. All group sessions are based on biblical principles. The group will meet (day/time) _____. Additionally, the Destined D.I.V.A. group may also attend special activities and outings. You will be notified in these instances, and asked to sign an outing permission/transportation release form for your teen to attend. We may take pictures/video during our meetings/outings that may be included in our church/organization's promotional materials. These pictures will not be abused in any way.

If you have any questions about this group or your teen's participation, please feel free to contact the D.I.V.A. group leader.

D.I.V.A. Leader: _____

Phone: _____

Email: _____

Please sign below indicating that (teen's name) _____ has your permission to participate in the D.I.V.A. group on the designated date and time.

Please initial here _____ to indicate that you authorize (church/organization) _____ to take images/video during the group activities for promotional purposes only. I understand that this consent has no time limitation, and that I may revoke my consent at any time in writing.

_____   _____
Parent/Guardian Name (please print)   Parent/Guardian Phone

_____   _____
Parent/Guardian Signature   Date

Note: This form is only a sample template for your convenience. Please have your church/organization's appropriate representative and/or legal counsel review this form to have the contents tailored to your specific needs and policies.

Become a Destined D.I.V.A.

Teen girls, ages 13-18 years old

Daughters of Integrity, Virtue, and Anointing

Church/Organization: _____

Day & Time: _____

Location: _____

* Learn about God * Talk abut REAL issues going on in YOUR life
* Ask questions without getting judged * Make friends

Questions? Call _____

Become a Destined D.I.V.A.

Teen girls, ages 13-18 years old

Daughters of Integrity, Virtue, and Anointing

Church/Organization: _____

Day & Time: _____

Location: _____

* Learn about God * Talk abut REAL issues going on in YOUR life
* Ask questions without getting judged * Make friends

Questions? Call _____

Become a Destined D.I.V.A.

Teen girls, ages 13-18 years old

Daughters of Integrity, Virtue, and Anointing

Church/Organization: _____

Day & Time: _____

Location: _____

* Learn about God * Talk abut REAL issues going on in YOUR life
* Ask questions without getting judged * Make friends

Questions? Call _____

Become a Destined D.I.V.A.

Teen girls, ages 13-18 years old

Daughters of Integrity, Virtue, and Anointing

Church/Organization: _____

Day & Time: _____

Location: _____

* Learn about God * Talk abut REAL issues going on in YOUR life
* Ask questions without getting judged * Make friends

Questions? Call _____

Donation Request

Church/Organization: _____

Dear: _____

The Destined D.I.V.A.s (Daughters of Integrity, Virtue, and Anointing) need your help!

Destined D.I.V.A. is a bible study group for girls; ages 13-18, with a focus on teaching life skills and biblical truths that will help young women make positive decisions that are aligned with their identity as children of God. The D.I.V.A. group meets (day & time) _____. In addition to engaging in bible studies, the girls that participate are also educated on life skill issues such as self-esteem, healthy relationships, sexual purity, goal setting, anger management, leadership, stress management, and several other topics.

We want the girls to get the most out of the group as possible, so we will be providing bibles and journals for girls participating in the group to encourage them to read and reflect on the scriptures and what they are learning in the group.

Additionally, we want to provide fellowship opportunities for the girls, so we will be planning fun outings and trips to keep them engaged. The outings assist in helping the girls grow closer together and to increase trust within the group in a fun setting. We also believe that the outings are an incentive for girls that have been coming consistently to the group to continue coming to learn about Jesus Christ, and His desire for a relationship with each of them. The girls, as well as the group facilitators, will be contributing to cover the cost of bibles and trips. However, your donation can also assist us in these efforts. Please help us if you can! Any amount is appreciated! Thank you for your consideration. If you have any questions, feel free to contact

_____.

- -

Name: _____   **Phone:** _____

Email: _____

☐ I will donate $_____ towards Destined D.I.V.A. Outings.

☐ I will donate $_____ towards bibles/journals for group participants.

☐ I cannot donate at this time. Please keep me updated on future opportunities to support the group.

- -

Note: This form is only a sample template for your convenience. Please have your church/organization's appropriate representative and/or legal counsel review this form to have the contents tailored to your specific needs and policies.

Outing Waiver & Transportation Release

Church/Organization: _____

Date: _____

To: Parent/Guardian of _____

From: _____

Your teen has been participating in the Destined D.I.V.A. group at our church/organization. Destined D.I.V.A. is a bible study group for girls, ages 13-18, with a focus on teaching life skills and biblical truths that will help young women make positive decisions that are aligned with their identity as children of God. In addition to engaging in bible studies and life skills training, the Destined D.I.V.A. group may also attend special activities and outings.

Trip Destination: _____

Location: _____

Date: _____

Transportation: The group will meet at (location) _____ at (time)_____ and carpool to the trip destination with the adult group facilitators/representatives. We will return to the pick-up location at approximately (time) _____.

Activities during the trip: _____

Fee: _____   **Due date for fee:** _____

If you have any questions about this outing, feel free to contact _____

- -

Please sign below indicating that (teen's name) _____ has your permission to attend the outing on the designated date and time, and to be transported via carpool with adult drivers who are licensed and insured. Your signature below indicates that you understand that there are certain risks associated with transportation to and from the activities described above, and that you release (church/organization) _____and its adult volunteers from any and all claims arising out of or in any way connected with your teen's participation in Destined D.I.V.A.

_____   _____
Parent/Guardian Name (please print)   Parent/Guardian Phone

_____   _____
Parent/Guardian Signature   Date

- -

Note: This form is only a sample template for your convenience. Please have your church/organization's appropriate representative and/or legal counsel review this form to have the contents tailored to your specific needs and policies.

D.I.V.A. Dollars

_____
Name

But you are a chosen people, a royal priesthood, a holy nation, God's special possession, that you may declare the praises of him who called you out of darkness into his wonderful light. (1Peter 2:9 NIV)

D.I.V.A. Dollars

_____
Name

But you are a chosen people, a royal priesthood, a holy nation, God's special possession, that you may declare the praises of him who called you out of darkness into his wonderful light. (1Peter 2:9 NIV)

D.I.V.A. Dollars

_____
Name

But you are a chosen people, a royal priesthood, a holy nation, God's special possession, that you may declare the praises of him who called you out of darkness into his wonderful light. (1Peter 2:9 NIV)

D.I.V.A. Dollars

_____
Name

But you are a chosen people, a royal priesthood, a holy nation, God's special possession, that you may declare the praises of him who called you out of darkness into his wonderful light. (1Peter 2:9 NIV)

D.I.V.A. Dollars

_____
Name

But you are a chosen people, a royal priesthood, a holy nation, God's special possession, that you may declare the praises of him who called you out of darkness into his wonderful light. (1Peter 2:9 NIV)

D.I.V.A. Dollars

_____
Name

But you are a chosen people, a royal priesthood, a holy nation, God's special possession, that you may declare the praises of him who called you out of darkness into his wonderful light. (1Peter 2:9 NIV)

D.I.V.A. Dollars

_____
Name

But you are a chosen people, a royal priesthood, a holy nation, God's special possession, that you may declare the praises of him who called you out of darkness into his wonderful light. (1Peter 2:9 NIV)

D.I.V.A. Dollars

_____
Name

But you are a chosen people, a royal priesthood, a holy nation, God's special possession, that you may declare the praises of him who called you out of darkness into his wonderful light. (1Peter 2:9 NIV)

ABOUT THE AUTHOR

Whether at work, volunteering in the community, or interacting with her family; Laura believes that every experience is an opportunity to minister to others and show God's love. Her first introduction to women's ministry was as the Women's Prayer Group leader during her college years. As a young woman who was seeking and growing in her own personal relationship with God, she helped her peers to remain steadfast in their faith while striving to strike a balance as college students. This experience sparked a passion in her for ministering to women and girls.

Laura would later go on to facilitate five more girl's empowerment groups over the years in both Christian settings and in secular settings as a social worker. After developing relationships with several teen girls in her church, she realized a need to work with those young women to help them learn about God's Word, His love, and how it could transform their life. She then started her first group under the "Destined D.I.V.A." title. Through this group, she began to see how the Lord was drawing the girls closer to Him, and how she was continuing to grow in her spiritual relationship with Him as she mentored and taught the girls. At the same time, she was praying for an entrepreneurial endeavor that will allow her to use her past skills and maintain her passion for serving women and girls. The Destined D.I.V.A. Leader's Guide and Handbook was birthed out of those prayers.

Through the D.I.V.A. system, Laura hopes to empower teen girls to let their light shine for Christ while providing a format to help adult women to mentor and model a "virtuous woman" example for them. The Destined D.I.V.A. system integrates practical life skills, group accountability, and biblical truths to help young women make positive decisions that are aligned with their identity as children of God.

In addition to her ministry work, Laura has been training youth and adults in the areas of job skill and life skill acquisition and strategy, and developing and managing programs to empower people for the last 12 years. She is a speaker, trainer, and consultant for groups, schools, businesses, and community organizations. She also works as a life coach to help individuals move beyond negative and limiting belief systems to overcome barriers and walk in their full potential. Laura's experience includes managing adult education and transitional jobs programs for low-income adults; developing, managing, and evaluating after-school and summer programs for youth, and working as a therapist to help families overcome various issues. She received her Bachelors of Science in Business Administration and Graduate Certificate in Non-profit Management from Washington University in St. Louis. Laura obtained her Master's in Social Work from DePaul University.

Laura is an active member at Mary Magdalene M.B. Church in Chicago, where she facilitates a Destined D.I.V.A. group. She lives in the South Suburbs of Illinois with her husband Marshall, and their daughter, Kai. To learn more about Laura and her work, visit www.lauraeknights.com.

Learn more about The Destined D.I.V.A. Lifestyle System, including new products and upcoming events, visit www.thedestineddivas.com.

Overview of The Destined D.I.V.A. Lifestyle System

Empowering women to mentor, encourage, and guide teen girls in the way of Christ

DESTINED D.I.V.A. LEADER'S GUIDE
****
* 25 Sessions
* Fun activities included
* Easy-to-follow
* Scriptures for each session
* Discussion prompts provided

D.I.V.A. LIVE!
SPEAKING, TRAINING & EVENTS
****
* D.I.V.A. Leader's Training
* D.I.V.A. Keynote Speaking for women and girls
* The D.I.V.A. Expo for teen girls
* D.I.V.A. Dialogue Sessions & Girls Night Out for adult women

THE D.I.V.A. HANDBOOK
****
* Devotional Journal for teen girls
* Use with D.I.V.A. groups or as stand alone item

D.I.V.A. APPAREL
****
Cute T-shirts with fun messages to share your love for Christ with the world!

Learn more at
www.thedestineddivas.com